REPORT OF THE CONSULTATIVE STEERING GROUP ON THE SCOTTISH PARLIAMENT

Presented to the
Secretary of State for Scotland

December 1998

More information on the Consultative Steering Group is available on The Scottish Office Devolution website

http://www.scottish-devolution.org.uk

Applications for reproductions should be made to HMSO

First published 1999

British Library Cataloguing in Publication Data

A catalogue record for this book is available from the British Library

ISBN 0 11 496125 5

CONTENTS

REPORT OF THE CONSULTATIVE STEERING GROUP ON THE SCOTTISH PARLIAMENT

FOREWORD

By CSG Chairman, Mr Henry McLeish MP, Scottish Office Minister of State, responsible for Home Affairs, Devolution and Local Government.

To the Secretary of State for Scotland,

It gives me tremendous satisfaction to present to you the Report of the Consultative Steering Group on the Scottish Parliament.

On behalf of the members of the Group I should like to thank you for giving us the opportunity to be involved in the challenge of drawing up detailed proposals on how the Scottish Parliament should operate. Our deliberations have been wide-ranging. We have consulted widely with interested bodies and individuals and we have been supported by expert advice from various panels established to aid our considerations.

In all our deliberations we have been struck by the degree of consensus that exists. In particular, that the establishment of the Scottish Parliament offers the opportunity to put in place a new sort of democracy in Scotland, closer to the Scottish people and more in tune with Scottish needs. People in Scotland have high hopes for their Parliament, and in developing our proposals we have been keen to ensure that these hopes will be met. In particular our recommendations envisage an open, accessible Parliament; a Parliament where power is shared with the people; where people are encouraged to participate in the policy making process which affects all our lives; an accountable, visible Parliament; and a Parliament which promotes equal opportunities for all.

I have been fortunate to chair a Group which has been open in its work and has striven throughout its deliberations to achieve consensus. I particularly welcome the constructive approaches taken by the representatives of the other main political parties in Scotland. This has allowed us to deliver a set of recommendations for a Parliament to which Scottish people can relate and in which they can take pride. The work of this Group has set the tone for the future of Scottish politics.

I would like to thank the members of the Group for the enthusiasm and commitment they have brought to this task. My thanks also go to the Scottish Office team who formed the Secretariat for their diligent work throughout the last 12 months.

We hope that this Report will stand as the blueprint for the manner in which the Scottish Parliament will operate and that it will provide a firm basis for the Standing Orders of the Parliament.

Henry McLeish MP

CONSULTATIVE STEERING GROUP: MEMBERSHIP AND REMIT

Members

Mr Henry McLeish MP, Minister of State (Chair)
Professor Alice Brown
Dr Campbell Christie CBE
Mr Andrew Cubie
Mr Paul Cullen QC
Mr Keith Geddes CBE
Mrs Deirdre Hutton CBE
Ms Joyce McMillan
Mr George Reid
Ms Esther Roberton
Dr Joan Stringer
Mr Jim Wallace QC MP
Canon Kenyon Wright

Remit

To bring together views on and consider the operational needs and working methods of the Scottish Parliament.

To develop proposals for the rules of procedure and Standing Orders which the Parliament might be invited to adopt.

To prepare a report to the Secretary of State by the end of 1998, to inform the preparation of draft Standing Orders.

Scottish Office Secretariat

Mr Robert Gordon, Head, Constitution Group
Mr John Ewing, Head, Constitutional Policy Division
Mr Murray Sinclair, Constitution Group Solicitors
Ms Carol McCracken, Head, Constitutional Policy Branch
Miss Jane McEwan, Constitutional Policy Branch
Ms Deborah Smith, Constitutional Policy Branch

SECTION ONE

INTRODUCTION

1. The Consultative Steering Group on the Scottish Parliament (CSG) was set up by the Secretary of State for Scotland in November 1997, following the positive outcome of the Scottish devolution referendum, and met for the first time in January 1998. Its membership included representatives of all four major Scottish political parties, as well as of a wide range of civic groups and interests; and our remit was both straightforward and daunting. It was:

> To bring together views on and consider the operational needs and working methods of the Scottish Parliament.
>
> To develop proposals for the rules of procedure and Standing Orders which the Parliament might be invited to adopt.
>
> To prepare a report to the Secretary of State by the end of 1998, to inform the preparation of Standing Orders.

2. The Government's White Paper "Scotland's Parliament"[1], published in July 1997, had already set out a broad framework for the operation of the new Parliament, drawing on the recommendations of the Scottish Constitutional Convention. It emphasised the Government's expectation that the Parliament would adopt modern methods of working; that it would be accessible, open and responsive to the needs of the public; that participation by organisations and individuals in decision-making would be encouraged; that views and advice from policy specialists would be sought as appropriate; and that Committees would play an important role in the new Parliament, able to initiate legislation, as well as to scrutinise and amend the Scottish Executive's proposals, carry out wide-ranging investigative functions, and meet regularly in locations away from Edinburgh, so as to improve public access to the Parliament's work.

3. The White Paper also stated the Government's wish, within these broad outlines, to leave detailed decisions on how the Scottish Parliament should operate to the Parliament itself. But it was clear from the outset that it would be unreasonable to expect MSPs to begin drawing up Standing Orders – the detailed operating rules of the Parliament – from scratch, immediately after the first elections. Hence the setting up of the CSG, with the task of developing a set of proposals which would be likely to command widespread support, and would provide a clear and well-founded basis for debate when the Parliament itself comes to make final decisions on its procedures and working methods.

4. In preparing its report, the CSG has therefore drawn on a wide range of information and advice: full details of our working methods, and of the results of our consultations, can be found in Annexes A-E. Our work was supported and administered throughout by a team of officials from The Scottish Office Constitution Group, who drafted the vast majority of our

---

1 Cm 3658.

1

working documents and papers. We were advised by the Expert Panels on Procedures and Standing Orders, Financial Issues, and Information and Communications Technologies, and by a Working Group on the Code of Conduct for MSPs; towards the end of the year, an Expert Panel on Media Issues was also set up.

5. In addition, we commissioned research into the working methods of national and regional Parliaments in the European Union and elsewhere. We launched a massive written (and electronic) public consultation exercise, actively inviting views on the working of the Parliament from more than 800 organisations, and placed copies of our papers and minutes on The Scottish Office Devolution Website for open public response. We used targeted focus groups to seek the views of groups often marginalised by consultation processes, including young people and people in urban, rural and remote areas; and we held a series of Open Forum meetings across Scotland, to allow us to hear views at first hand.

6. In presenting this report to the Secretary of State, and to the wider Scottish public, we would therefore like to thank everyone who took part in this consultation process, and in the development of our thinking about the kind of Parliament Scotland will need in the 21st century. The remainder of the report is divided into 3 sections.

Section 2 outlines the key principles which we determined should guide our work, and describes how those principles shaped our thinking about the practical operation of the Parliament.

Section 3 contains more detailed proposals for procedures and Standing Orders which we believe embody those principles, and would help to give them real force in Scotland's political life.

Section 4 outlines how our work will be taken forward.

7. Our aim has been to try to capture, in the nuts and bolts of Parliamentary procedure, some of the high aspirations for a better, more responsive and more truly democratic system of government that have informed the movement for constitutional change in Scotland; and in submitting these proposals for debate, our hope is that the principles on which they have been based will continue to influence the life of Scotland's Parliament, not only in the letter of its Standing Orders, but in the spirit of its work.

THE KEY PRINCIPLES: PUTTING THEM INTO PRACTICE

1. The background to the establishment of the Consultative Steering Group on the Scottish Parliament is set out in the preceding section and in Annexes A-E. They record how we approached our remit, including details of the wide-ranging consultation exercise which we undertook. This section focuses on the key principles which guided our work and shows how we have sought to give them effect in our recommendations.

Key Principles

2. We adopted the following key principles to guide our work:

- the Scottish Parliament should embody and reflect the sharing of power between the people of Scotland, the legislators and the Scottish Executive;

- the Scottish Executive should be accountable to the Scottish Parliament and the Parliament and Executive should be accountable to the people of Scotland;

- the Scottish Parliament should be accessible, open, responsive, and develop procedures which make possible a participative approach to the development, consideration and scrutiny of policy and legislation;

- the Scottish Parliament in its operation and its appointments should recognise the need to promote equal opportunities for all.

3. These key principles were an invaluable benchmark against which to test our emerging conclusions. They also served as a basis for the consultation exercise and have been broadly welcomed and accepted by the wide range of bodies and individuals who have responded to us. We invite the Scottish Parliament to endorse them, to stand as a symbol of what the Scottish people may reasonably expect from their elected representatives.

4. These key principles and our recommendations are also designed to achieve the Parliament envisaged by the Scottish Constitutional Convention, in the Government's White Paper "Scotland's Parliament" and provided for in the Scotland Act 1998 (referred to throughout as the Scotland Act). They aim to provide an open, accessible and, above all, participative Parliament, which will take a proactive approach to engaging with the Scottish people - in particular those groups traditionally excluded from the democratic process. To achieve this the Scottish Parliament must avoid adopting procedures which are obscure or archaic. It should adopt procedures and practices that people will understand, that will engage their interest, and that will encourage them to obtain information and exchange views. We have detected a great deal of cynicism about and disillusionment with the democratic process; it will require an effort both from the Parliament itself and from the people with whom it interacts to achieve the participative democracy many seek. We

firmly believe that the Scottish Parliament should set itself the highest standards. Our key principles are intended to achieve a Parliament whose elected Members the Scottish people will trust and respect, and a Parliament with which they will want to engage.

Key Principles into Practice (1): Sharing the Power

- **the Scottish Parliament should embody and reflect the sharing of power between the people of Scotland, the legislators and the Scottish Executive.**

5. There are a number of aspects of Parliamentary business which are relevant to our first key principle. These include the way Parliamentary business is programmed, the role of the Presiding Officer, the role of Committees, the role of civic society and public petitions.

The Programming of Parliamentary Business

6. We believe that the arrangements for the programming of business in the Scottish Parliament should be inclusive and transparent, and should provide reasonable time for business initiated by non-Executive parties, by individual Members and by Committees, and for Committee work. We believe that any arrangements for planning the business of the Parliament need to balance the potentially conflicting demands for time in Plenary session and in Committee which will arise. They must:

6.1 recognise the need for the Executive to govern, including enacting primary and subordinate legislation and obtaining approval of its expenditure proposals;

6.2 provide Parliament with the time and opportunity to scrutinise the work of the Executive;

6.3 allow for the debate of issues of both national and local interest;

6.4 enable individual Members to raise matters of concern and introduce proposals for legislation;

6.5 allow sufficient time for Committees to carry out their work.

7. We therefore support the model used in many Parliaments in Europe and beyond whereby the business of the Parliament is planned in a Business Committee, chaired by the Presiding Officer, comprising representatives of the political groups, to develop in a transparent, and, insofar as possible, consensual, way proposals for the programme of business of the Parliament. Our detailed recommendations are set out in section 3.3.

The Role of the Presiding Officer

8. We have given considerable thought to the role of the Presiding Officer, as this will be a key post in the Scottish Parliament. We believe that the Presiding Officer must be able to command the respect of the whole Parliament. The Presiding Officer's authority must be respected at all times to preserve the dignity of the Parliament and the integrity of the Office. In addition to the functions prescribed in the Scotland Act, we propose a number of other functions which, taken together, will mean that the Presiding Officer will, in performing his or her role, have considerable influence on the operation of the Parliament and on the way the Parliament is perceived. To achieve and maintain that respect, it is essential that the Presiding Officer acts, and is seen to act, even-handedly, with impartiality

and protecting the rights of all MSPs. The need to preserve impartiality has implications for the extent to which the Presiding Officer, and his/her Deputies, should be allowed to participate in the proceedings of the Parliament. Our detailed recommendations are set out in section 3.2.

Sharing the Power: the Role of Parliamentary Committees

9. The White Paper "Scotland's Parliament" signalled the Government's intention that Committees would have an important role to play in the work of the Parliament. It envisaged that these Committees might, for example, initiate legislation, scrutinise and amend the Scottish Executive's proposals, and have wide-ranging investigative functions. Such a role for the Committees would ensure that the legislative and policy proposals of the Executive would receive appropriate scrutiny. The White Paper also indicated that the Committees might meet from time-to-time at locations throughout Scotland so that people in all parts of Scotland could see how their Parliamentarians worked and interact with them. It was against this background, and the background of the Scottish Constitutional Convention's proposals for a Scottish Parliament with a strong Committee structure, that we conducted our deliberations.

10. We propose that the Scottish Parliament should have the capacity in Committees:

- to consider and report on the policy and administration of the Scottish Administration;

- to conduct inquiries into such matters or issues as the Parliament may require;

- to scrutinise primary and secondary legislation and proposed European Union legislation;

- to initiate legislation;

- to scrutinise financial proposals and administration of the Scottish Executive (including variation of taxes, estimates, appropriation and audit); and

- to scrutinise procedures relating to the Parliament and its Members (including adherence to those procedures).

11. In all cases, Committees should report to the Parliament with recommendations.

12. There are a few Committees which Standing Orders should require to be established, including a Business Committee, an Audit Committee and a Procedures Committee (see section 3.2). Their functions and maximum size should be prescribed in Standing Orders. Beyond that, Standing Orders should set out certain basic criteria for Committees, such as a maximum membership, a quorum and arrangements for deciding membership.

13. On the shape of the Committee structure we recommend that the Scottish Parliament should have all-purpose Committees, combining the Westminster Select and Standing Committee role. This would enable Members to develop an expertise in particular areas and to bring an informed view to the consideration of legislation and scrutiny of the Executive.

14. We believe that the Parliament needs to be able to address cross-cutting issues, and to ensure that matters which cross conventional departmental boundaries are properly

handled. We recognise the benefits of a Scottish Parliament structure coinciding with the structure of the Scottish Executive, which would facilitate close scrutiny of Executive actions and in particular of financial matters. We support the proposal made in some submissions to us that the Parliament should be able to establish ad hoc Committees to look at cross-cutting issues as required (public health, social inclusion and environmental sustainability were cited as 3 possible examples). Additionally, Committees should be empowered to conduct joint meetings and inquiries.

15. We considered the model of the reporter (or "rapporteur") used in many continental Parliaments. The reporter shares with the Committee Convener the responsibility for supervising the progress of deliberations on a particular issue, drawing up the results of deliberations on the topic in question and preparing the Committee's report to the Plenary. The role of the reporter is essentially a political one, with the reporter leading the Committee's discussions and identifying the key issues which need to be considered.

16. We concluded that Standing Orders should be left sufficiently broad to allow, but not compel, Committees to appoint a reporter who might fulfil a similar role in the Scottish Parliament, both in respect of consideration of Bills, and in respect of Committee inquiries. We recommend (section 3.2) that Committees should be encouraged to appoint reporters, who, among other things, would act as a focal point for interest groups and individuals who wish to make representations to the Committee, and who would seek to identify consensus.

Sharing the Power: the Role of Civic Society

17. Power-sharing is not only about the balance of power between the Scottish Executive and the Scottish Parliament, but also about the empowerment of external groups and individuals in all sectors of Scottish society.

18. An important section of our recommendations deals with the policy-making and law-making process. A key feature of the comments made to us was the concern expressed that individuals and organisations find it difficult to inform and influence the policy-making process. In particular in the case of legislation it was felt that the opportunity to influence legislation was limited after it had been introduced; and that the consultation process leading up to the introduction was ineffective, in part because the detailed content of the draft legislation was often not known until a Bill was introduced to Parliament. Our recommendations, therefore, envisage a process which involves genuine participation and consultation led by the Executive with greater use of draft Bills, and with the potential for further evidence-taking by Committees of the Parliament. It will be important for both the Executive and the Parliament to take full account of the views of those most likely to be affected in their consideration of policy or legislative proposals. Our proposals are set out in section 3.5.

19. The development and implementation of legislation needs to take account of the diversity which exists across Scotland. Specifically, we recognise that well intentioned legislation cannot always be implemented in an Islands context without practical difficulties arising. The open and consultative approach of the Parliament (including the use of IT) should enhance the opportunities for any perceived difficulties to be addressed at an early stage. We recommend that Committees engaged in pre-legislative scrutiny should specifically address the issue of implementation in Islands areas and where appropriate make recommendations for suitable amendments or derogations. The Parliament should

also consider mechanisms to provide for prompt amendment of legislation, where unforeseen difficulties in implementation emerge in Islands areas.

20. It is important that our proposals for a more open political process are paralleled by the development of appropriate institutions at different levels in Scottish society, to ensure meaningful dialogue between the Parliament and civic society. In this respect, we welcome proposals which were presented to us for a Civic Forum, which would be facilitative, recognise the plurality of voices and groups and take an active role in ensuring the effective involvement of groups traditionally excluded from the decision-making process. We endorse the proposals for a Civic Forum and encourage the proponents of such a Forum to develop the details of the role and funding arrangements for the Forum. We recommend that the Parliament should encourage Scottish civic society through the establishment and work of a Civic Forum and through other imaginative social partnership ventures. We see these as significant means of achieving an accessible Parliament within a participative democracy. Our endorsement of this proposal does not, of course, exclude the use of other means of engaging with the Parliament. It is important also to recognise the plurality of voices which exists in Scottish civic society and the establishment of a Civic Forum would not preclude the development of other social partnership ventures. Details of other means of communicating are outlined in Annex G and we recommend that the Parliament considers how these might best be used to achieve greater public participation.

Public Petitions

21. It is important to enable groups and individuals to influence the Parliament's agenda. We looked at a number of models in other Parliaments for handling petitions and concluded that the best of these encouraged petitions; had clear and simple rules as to form and content; and specified clear expectations of how petitions would be handled.

22. It is important to establish a strong system for handling petitions from the outset. We propose the establishment of a dedicated Petitions Committee, our detailed proposals for which are set out in section 3.6.

Key Principles into Practice (2): Accountability

- **the Scottish Executive should be accountable to the Scottish Parliament and the Parliament and Executive should be accountable to the people of Scotland.**

Members

23. One of the keys to the success of the Scottish Parliament will be the extent to which its Members embrace the new culture. The Scottish Office is putting in place a wide-ranging induction training programme for MSPs and we believe that it is important that this should include helping MSPs to make the Parliament a success in terms of openness, accessibility and participation and accountability of Members to their constituents.

24. The Scottish people deserve a Parliament and Members they can trust and respect. We were pleased to be invited by the Secretary of State to consider how the highest standards might be achieved in the Scottish Parliament. We recommend a rigorous Code of Conduct for MSPs. Section 3.2 sets out our recommendations for a set of key principles

which should govern such a Code: the preparation of detailed proposals for the Code is being taken forward by the Code of Conduct Working Group, and will be the subject of a supplementary report in Spring 1999.

Scottish Executive

25.   We have been careful to develop procedures designed to ensure that the Scottish Executive is fully accountable to the Scottish Parliament for its actions. Our proposals include a strong role for Committees and a system of Parliamentary Questions, which will enable individual MSPs to address questions to the Executive. Our recommendations are described in section 3.4.

Finance

26.   The Scottish Parliament should have rigorous financial systems and audit arrangements in place to facilitate proper scrutiny of expenditure of the Scottish Block. Our proposals on the financial arrangements for the Parliament are set out in section 3.4 and Annex I.

Europe

27.   The Scottish Parliament needs arrangements in place to facilitate proper scrutiny of draft European legislation and other developments in Europe. We propose the establishment of a Committee dedicated to considering European issues, together with a strong role for relevant subject Committees. Our detailed proposals are set out in section 3.4.

Key Principles into Practice (3): Access and Participation

-   **the Scottish Parliament should be accessible, open, responsive and develop procedures which make possible a participative approach to the development, consideration and scrutiny of policy and legislation.**

28.   Access to the Scottish Parliament is a cornerstone of our recommendations. It has implications for all of the issues we considered and has influenced all of our recommendations. For the Scottish Parliament to deliver a Parliament which will meet the expectations of the Scottish people, a culture of openness and accessibility has to permeate the Parliament, from the way Committees operate (section 3.2), to the provision of information through a professional public information service, the use of IT (section 3.6), the passage of legislation (section 3.5), the planning of the business of the Parliament (section 3.3) etc.   Since the Scottish Executive will be responsible for the distribution of most of the Parliament's £15 billion budget and for implementing policies and developing legislation in Scotland, we believe that it is essential that the culture of openness and accessibility is reflected in the working of the Scottish Executive. While our remit is limited to looking at how the Scottish Parliament might operate, it is clear when we consider the responsibilities which lie with the Scottish Executive, that the way it operates will have considerable influence on the way the Scottish Parliament is perceived. Where it has been possible we have addressed this in our recommendations. But we would draw to the attention of the Parliament the considerable pressure which it can, and in our view should, exert to ensure that the Scottish Executive reflects our expectations for the Parliament.

29.   We considered 8 key issues related to accessibility and participation. These are:

- how the Parliament and the Executive might consult on issues;

- how to encourage wide participation in the work of the Parliament;

- how to facilitate participation in the work of Committees;

- how to facilitate transparency;

- how to use information and communications technologies to achieve an accessible Parliament;

- how the Parliament might provide information;

- how the physical accommodation might be made accessible;

- pastoral issues.

Consultation Mechanisms

30.   We believe that while most consultation mechanisms we have examined are potentially attractive, there will always be need to exercise judgement as to what will be most effective in particular circumstances.   It will be important for the Parliament to provide different channels for consultation and to review and assess the effectiveness of particular approaches, some of which are set out in Annex G.

Access: Encouraging Wide Participation

31.   As noted in paragraph 18, our recommendations include proposals for a pre-legislative, policy development phase. In particular we recommend that Executive Bills should complete a consultative process before being presented to the Parliament.   On introduction a Bill should be accompanied by a comprehensive memorandum explaining the nature of the problem it is intended to address, and the strategic approach; the options considered and why the particular option was chosen; the consultative process undertaken; the best estimates of costs and benefits; and other possible matters such as sustainable development, human rights, Islands issues.   The Bill on introduction would be considered at first by the relevant Committee, which would consider and report on the general principles of the Bill, to inform a debate and vote on the principles of the Bill in the Plenary session.   At this stage the Committee would also be able to comment on the memorandum accompanying the Bill, and could recommend whether further evidence should be taken to inform the detailed consideration of the Bill.   Our detailed recommendations are contained in section 3.5.

32.   It will also be important to develop a culture of genuine consultation and participation if people in Scotland, particularly those who do not currently engage in the political process, are to be encouraged to participate. This will require not only a degree of education about how groups and individuals might play a role but also a properly developed and resourced system for making issues accessible to non-experts and providing feedback to those who do respond. This applies equally to the Scottish Executive and the Scottish Parliament.

33. To achieve a participative Parliament requires an effort both from the Parliament itself and from the people with whom it interacts. We were interested to note that many responses to our consultation exercise proposed civic education as a means of raising awareness of the democratic process at an early stage. We are pleased to note that the arrangements being put in place for the Parliament include a Parliamentary information centre, with an education centre and education officer. We also understand that The Scottish Office is taking forward arrangements for the preparation of educational material on the Scottish Parliament, informing people about the democratic structures in Scotland.

34. We believe that young people should be given every encouragement and opportunity to make their voices heard. We would strongly encourage schools to make full use of educational material to inform the young people of Scotland about the democratic structures in Scotland, their relevance and their relationship to them. Teachers should be involved in the development of appropriate materials. Thought should also be given to the development of consultative structures both locally and nationally. One of the most exciting aspects of our consultation process was the workshops which we held with young people from around Scotland, organised on our behalf by the Scottish Community Education Council. The suggestions that they made included proposals for a Youth Parliament; a Scottish Parliament which addresses young people's concerns; and the hope that information on the Scottish Parliament would be disseminated through a more imaginative use of media such as television and magazines. We endorse these views, and very much hope that the Parliament will take heed of them.

35. Concern has also been expressed over the negative portrayal of politics by the media. The media has the potential to play an important positive role in explaining how the Parliament operates and helping to facilitate its consultative processes.

Access: the Role of Committees

36. The role of Committees in achieving an accessible Parliament is very important.

Access: Location of Committees

37. We recognise that the Parliament must be a Parliament for the whole of Scotland - not just for Edinburgh. This was a key concern arising from our consultation exercise. In particular, we realise that it is likely that credence will only be given to this commitment if the Parliament actively involves other areas of Scotland. We propose that Committees should be encouraged to meet and to take evidence outside Edinburgh, particularly when the subject matter might affect people staying in a particular area of Scotland, and that in a number of cases Committees should have their permanent base somewhere other than Edinburgh.

Access: the Role of Committees in Gathering Views

38. Committees would be expected to take the views of interested bodies when examining policy matters, conducting inquiries or considering legislation. The precise mechanisms will vary from case to case. This might be facilitated through formal consultation structures associated with each Committee, which would act as a focus for consultation, or through the recognition of particular forums such as a Civic Forum, Business Forum, Transport Forum, Youth Forum. Whichever umbrella organisations were established, it would be important to enable single groups or individuals also to access the Committees.

39.   In response to our consultation there was some support for the idea of allowing Committees to establish one or more Expert Panels, of varying duration, in which non-Members could advise on areas in which they hold particular expertise. Advice from the Expert Panels would be considered by the Committee, together with all other views and evidence. Such a system would be similar to the support provided to CSG by the various Expert Panels which we found to work effectively. We recommend that Committees should be empowered to establish such panels. Rules governing appointments to such panels would have to be carefully drawn up, to ensure that appointments were made on merit and reflected a comprehensive range of opinion and expertise.

40.   The proposal has also been made that Committees should be able to co-opt non-MSPs as non-voting members so that their expertise can be made available. Whenever appropriate we recommend that Committees should consider this option, and that Standing Orders should permit this.

41.   In summary it is clear that there is no single model for consultation, participation and involvement which is appropriate in every case. The Parliament should be invited to encourage its Committees to adopt different mechanisms appropriate to the issue under consideration.

Access: Facilitating Transparency

42.   In its day to day business, the Parliament should be transparent, modern and adopt simple working practices. We recommend that the Parliament should observe normal business hours, and that proceedings should normally be in public. Members should refer to each other by name. The Parliament should be committed to the use of plain English in its proceedings and its publications. We would also encourage the production of regular information bulletins about the Parliament in English and in other languages in use in Scotland.

Access: the Use of Information and Communications Technologies

43.   Use of IT and other information media will also be an important factor in ensuring that people all across Scotland are able to gain access to and information on the processes of the Parliament. The Expert Panel on Information and Communications Technologies identified a wide range of exciting options for achieving an accessible, participative Parliament.   Our proposals for Information and Communications Technologies are contained in section 3.6; a summary of the recommendations of the ICT Panel's sub-group on democratic participation is set out in Annex J.

Access: Providing Information

44.   An important part of our deliberations focused on the provision of a Parliamentary information centre. We were impressed by the high quality service provided by the Swedish Parliament, and noted that this was founded upon an Information Strategy which had been endorsed by the Swedish Parliament. Annex F sets out a draft Information Strategy which we would invite the Scottish Parliament to endorse as a blueprint for its own information activities.

Access: Physical Accommodation

45.   We hope that the physical environment and atmosphere of the Parliament will provide an ethos of public access to and ownership of the Parliament. We suggest that a physical form, such as a touchstone sculpture or object in the Parliament's main public space would provide an appropriate symbol of the people's right of access to the Parliament.

Access: Pastoral Issues

46.   We welcomed the proposals made to us in a submission by Action of Churches Together in Scotland (ACTS) on the level and nature of pastoral support from an interfaith chaplaincy team which might be provided to MSPs and staff in the Scottish Parliament, including proposals that there should be a regular prayer/other spiritual meditation/reflection period built into the life of the Parliament. We recommend that the Parliament should reach an early view on these issues.

Key Principles into Practice (4): Equal Opportunities

-   **the Scottish Parliament in its operation and its appointments should recognise the need to promote equal opportunities for all.**

47.   Our fourth key principle is that the Scottish Parliament should recognise the need to allow equal opportunities for all. Equal opportunities should be mainstreamed into the work of the Parliament, and through the demands of and scrutiny by the Parliament, into the work of the Executive. Mainstreaming has been defined by the Equal Opportunities Commission as the integration of equal opportunities into all policy development, legislation, implementation, evaluation and review practices (see Annex H).

Committees

48.   We considered whether Committees of the Scottish Parliament could reasonably be expected to mainstream equal opportunities considerations in all their work, or whether a further mechanism was needed to ensure that such mainstreaming is delivered. We recommend that there should be an Equal Opportunities Committee (see section 3.2) and that an Equality Unit should also be established to provide a focus for these efforts. The role of the Committee would be to act as a catalyst to ensure that, for instance, equality plans and targets are outlined for each Committee and effective monitoring systems are put in place by Committees. Crucially, this would ensure a proper focus on equality issues during the early years of the Parliament's life while the skills and expertise necessary for effective mainstreaming are being developed by all MSPs and officials. To ensure the effectiveness of mainstreaming it will be necessary for all MSPs and for all officials to receive training on equal opportunities with the emphasis on policy appraisal. The aim should be to achieve effective mainstreaming. We believe that an Equal Opportunities Committee has a crucial role to play in ensuring that the Parliament begins operating in a way that will enable it to comply with our important fourth principle.

Working Pattern

49.   We agreed the following main principles which we believe should govern the working pattern of the Scottish Parliament:

- the sitting pattern of the Parliament should be "family friendly";

- the arrangements for the operation of the Parliament should be equally attractive to men and women; and

- the Parliament should meet during normal business hours on a regular, programmed basis.

50. Our proposals for the sitting pattern of the Parliament are set out in section 3.3.

Language

51. We believe that it is important for the language used in Parliamentary proceedings and papers to be as simple, clear, inclusive and non-gender specific as possible. This would make an important contribution towards meeting all 4 of our key principles.

Self Assessment And Monitoring

Measuring Effectiveness

52. The recommendations in this section all flow from our 4 key principles: power-sharing; accountability; access and participation; and equal opportunities which we hope the Parliament will endorse and adopt. We recommend that the Parliament should regularly review its policy and performance against these key principles. We suggest that such reviews should be undertaken at least once during each Parliamentary session; with the end of each Parliament providing a further opportunity to take stock. This might be an appropriate role for the Procedures Committee as it relates to the procedures of the Parliament and how the Parliament interacts with the Scottish people, and for the Equal Opportunities Committee in relation to the implementation of the fourth key principle.

Conclusion

53. This section of our report sets out the way in which we believe the Scottish Parliament should operate and the implications of this for Scotland as a whole. We see the Parliament as the central institution of a new political and community culture, and recognise that a more open democracy requires innovative institutions and attitudes in Scottish society, if our goal of a participative approach to the development, consideration and scrutiny of policy and legislation is to be achieved. While these aspirations cannot all be directly reflected in the Standing Orders, we feel strongly that the Standing Orders should be drafted with these expectations and implications in mind, and should encourage the Parliament to operate as we propose. The remainder of this report sets out our proposals in more detail and includes proposals on the technical aspects of procedure which must be included in Standing Orders. For more detail of the reasoning behind our proposals, CSG papers and notes of our meetings can be found on The Scottish Office Devolution Website, www.scottish-devolution.org.uk, together with a summary list of decisions taken by the Group.

SECTION THREE

DETAILED RECOMMENDATIONS

SECTION 3.1:

THE STANDING ORDERS FOR THE SCOTTISH PARLIAMENT

1. From its very first meeting, the Parliament's proceedings will be governed by its Standing Orders. It is through these that the type of Parliament envisaged in our key principles can be achieved. The Standing Orders will have a significant influence. In the various chapters of this section we set out our detailed recommendations, developed against the background of our four key principles.

Scotland Act 1998

2. The Scotland Act provides that the proceedings of the Parliament should be regulated by Standing Orders. It prescribes certain matters which must be provided for within Standing Orders. It does not prescribe how Standing Orders should be made or amended.

Standing Orders

3. As part of our remit, we were charged with reporting to the Secretary of State for Scotland with proposals for the Standing Orders for the Scottish Parliament. We understand that on the basis of the advice contained in our report, the Secretary of State will prescribe in subordinate legislation made under the transitional provisions of the Scotland Act the first Standing Orders of the Scottish Parliament.

4. We believe that the Standing Orders of the Parliament should be written in as simple language as possible, to facilitate a wider understanding of the Parliament's procedures.

5. We recommend that any elected Member should be able to propose a change to the Standing Orders: proposals would be submitted to the Procedures Committee (see section 3.2) which would take a view and make a recommendation to the Parliament. A final decision should be taken by the Parliament. A minimum period should be required between the Committee's recommendation and the Plenary vote.

6. To build in a period of stability, we recommend that initially Standing Orders should be able to be changed only with an absolute majority of the Parliament (ie a majority of the total number of seats in the Parliament, or 65 votes out of 129 Members). (Any amendment to the Standing Orders would, of course, have to be made within the parameters set out in the Scotland Act, for example, in relation to exclusion of Members.) The Parliament would be able to change this arrangement in the light of experience if it wished, subject to observing the requirements of the Scotland Act. The proposals contained in this report, however, are not intended to be restraining: they are designed to allow the Parliament to grow and develop.

7. We recommend that changes to Standing Orders, once agreed by the Parliament, should take effect immediately, unless the Parliament resolves otherwise.

8. Subject to observing the provisions of the Scotland Act, Standing Orders should be able to be suspended. Any member should be able to propose that a Standing Order should be suspended, provided that prior notice is given.

Summary of recommendations for Standing Orders

Standing Orders should:

- enable any Member to propose a change to Standing Orders;

- provide that such proposals should be submitted to the Procedures Committee, which should make a recommendation to the Parliament. A final decision should be taken by the Parliament;

- require that a minimum period should be allowed between the Committee's recommendation and the final decision;

- provide that Standing Orders should be able to be changed only with an absolute majority of the Parliament;

- provide that changes to Standing Orders once agreed by the Parliament should take effect immediately, unless the Parliament resolves otherwise;

- provide that Standing Orders should be able to be suspended: any Member should be able to propose that a Standing Order should be suspended, provided that he or she gives prior notice.

SECTION 3.2:

ISSUES RELATING TO MEMBERS, OFFICES AND BODIES OF THE PARLIAMENT

1. This section considers matters relating to the Presiding Officer, the Scottish Executive, Scottish Law Officers, Members, the Scottish Parliamentary Corporate Body and Committees of the Parliament.

The Presiding Officer

2. The Scotland Act provides (section 19, sub-sections (1), (2) and (3)) that:

(1) The Parliament shall, at its first meeting following a general election, elect from among its Members a Presiding Officer and two Deputies.

(2) A person elected Presiding Officer or Deputy shall hold office until the conclusion of the next election for Presiding Officer under sub-section (1), unless he previously resigns, ceases to be a Member of the Parliament otherwise than by virtue of a dissolution or is removed from office by resolution of the Parliament.

(3) If the Presiding Officer or a Deputy ceases to hold office before the Parliament is dissolved, the Parliament shall elect another from among its Members to fill his place.

3. We propose that where there is no Presiding Officer, the oldest Member in the Parliament, who is not a candidate for the posts of Presiding Officer, Deputy Presiding Officer or First Minister, should preside over the election of the Presiding Officer or Deputy.

4. While it will be for MSPs themselves to elect their Presiding Officer, we believe that it is important to specify as far as possible the main functions of the post, so that MSPs may make an informed choice as to the most suitable candidate for the job.

5. We propose that the main functions of the Presiding Officer should be:

- to be politically impartial, taking the interests of all Members equally into account;

- to preside over the proceedings of the Scottish Parliament in the Plenary session, exercising a casting vote in the event of a tie;

- to apply and give rulings on Standing Orders;

- to chair the Business Committee, which would prepare proposals for the Scottish Parliament on the agenda, organisation of business etc;

- to take decisions on the legislative competence of draft Bills; to submit Bills for Royal Assent, and other functions associated with the legislative process;

- to represent the Parliament in interactions with the Scottish Administration; the UK Parliament; and the devolved Assemblies in Northern Ireland and Wales and any inter-Parliamentary bodies associated with them;

- to represent the Scottish Parliament in interactions with other Parliaments and Assemblies furth of the United Kingdom.

Other Functions

6. We have proposed a number of other detailed functions for the Presiding Officer to which we refer in the relevant sections. For example, we propose that the Presiding Officer should have considerable discretion over the control of conduct in the Chamber, and in applying rules of debate etc. We propose a role for the Presiding Officer in relation to sub judice, and a role in relation to exclusion of both Members and non-Members from proceedings. In every case we have taken into account the dignity of the office, and the need to preserve the impartiality of the Presiding Officer.

Impartiality

7. To preserve the impartiality of the office, we propose that the Presiding Officer should not take part in proceedings of the Parliament (eg participate in debates, ask Parliamentary Questions), and should have only a casting vote. We suggest that the casting vote might be, as it is in Westminster, a vote to have the matter reconsidered, or a vote for the status quo, to avoid the Presiding Officer becoming embroiled in political controversy. However, Standing Orders should provide only for a casting vote; the conventions surrounding its use would develop over time.

8. While we believe that it is important for the Presiding Officer in the chair to be seen as above party politics, we recognise, however, that due regard must be given to ensuring that, in a Parliament of 129 MSPs, there is a sufficient pool of MSPs willing to stand for the positions of Deputy Presiding Officers (DPOs). If DPOs were to be precluded from voting at any time (except when using the chair's casting vote), this could act as a disincentive to Members who wished to be able to vote on the business of the Parliament when not presiding. In considering this issue, we noted that most Deputy Presiding Officers or equivalents in continental Parliaments are able to participate and vote when not presiding. Provided that, when in the chair, they are seen to act impartially, this does not appear to give rise to difficulties. We recommend that there should be no restrictions on the DPOs' powers to participate in debate or to vote unless they are presiding over the business of the Parliament at the time.

9. We recommend that at the first stage of the election of the Presiding Officer, nominations, which should be seconded, should be made from the Plenary. A set period should be allowed for such nominations to be made. A successful candidate would be given the opportunity to speak to accept election after the vote.

10. Nominations may be made only at the beginning of the process, not between successive votes.

11. A ballot should be held, overseen by the Clerk and 2 scrutineers drawn by lots from the Members who are not candidates.

12. If there are more than 2 candidates, the candidate receiving the fewest number of votes in the first ballot should drop out, and successive ballots should be held until a clear winning candidate has been identified.

13. The winning candidate should command the support of a simple majority of Members voting, subject to a quorum for the number of Members voting of 25% of all the seats in the Parliament.

14. If a clear winner is not identified, the process should begin afresh.

15. The DPOs should be elected successively after the Presiding Officer. We would expect MSPs to have regard to our fourth key principle, equal opportunities, in nominating candidates. If the Presiding Officer and first Deputy Presiding Officer elected came from the same political party, then nominations for the second Deputy Presiding Officer should not be allowed for candidates from that party.

16. The Presiding Officer and the Deputies may resign at any time. The Deputy Presiding Officers should intimate resignation to the Presiding Officer, who should announce the resignation to Parliament. The Presiding Officer should announce his/her resignation to Parliament. Resignations would be published.

17. Standing Orders should provide for a maximum period of 14 sitting days between the resignation of a Presiding Officer or Deputy Presiding Officer and the holding of an election for a successor.

18. The Presiding Officer may be removed from office only by an absolute majority of the number of seats in the Parliament: ie, at least 65 votes in favour of removal would be required. The same should apply to Deputy Presiding Officers.

19. The voting rights of the Presiding Officer should be restricted to a casting vote. The Presiding Officer should not be able to participate in proceedings of the Parliament, other than to fulfil the functions imposed on him/her in the Scotland Act and proposed in this report.

20. The Presiding Officer should be able to delegate any of his/her functions to the Deputy Presiding Officers, subject to the provisions of the Scotland Act.

21. There should be no restrictions on the Deputy Presiding Officers' powers to participate or to vote, unless they are presiding over the business of the Parliament at the time.

22. Deputy Presiding Officers should be allowed to make a casting vote when they are presiding.

The Scottish Executive

Scotland Act

23. Sections 44-50 of the Scotland Act provide for the Scottish Executive. They prescribe the way in which the Executive should be appointed and removed from office, and make associated provisions.

Appointment of the First Minister

24.   The appointment of the First Minister will have 3 main stages:

- nomination of a candidate by the Parliament;

- recommendation of the nominated candidate by the Presiding Officer to Her Majesty The Queen for appointment;

- appointment of the First Minister by Her Majesty The Queen.

25.   Any MSP, provided they are supported by a proposer and a seconder, should be able to stand for nomination for First Minister. The names of candidates should be submitted to the Presiding Officer. Following this an election or series of elections would take place by means of a roll call vote of MSPs, in which names should be progressively eliminated until one candidate emerged who enjoyed the support of a simple majority of MSPs. A quorum for voting, equal to 25% of the total number of seats, would be required. The successful candidate would then be recommended by the Presiding Officer to Her Majesty The Queen for appointment.

Scottish Ministers

26.   The Scotland Act provides that once the First Minister has been appointed by The Queen, he or she may, with the agreement of the Parliament and with Her Majesty's approval, appoint Scottish Ministers. Before seeking The Queen's approval of any appointment the First Minister must obtain the agreement of the Parliament.

27.   We propose that Standing Orders should remain flexible enough to allow the First Minister to seek the Parliament's approval of the proposals for appointment of Scottish Ministers either individually or *en bloc*. In any case Standing Orders should provide a mechanism for agreeing to the appointment of individual Ministers in the case of resignations, and other contingencies.

28.   Agreement to these appointments should be sought on the basis of an amendable motion to enable the Parliament to reject, but not to substitute, particular individuals included in the list submitted by the First Minister should it wish to do so. As the power of appointment lies with the First Minister it would not be appropriate to allow Parliament to add names to the list. A simple majority of those voting, subject to a quorum for voting equal to 25% of the total number of seats, would be required to secure the Parliament's agreement to the motion. We note that the allocation of portfolios to Ministers would be a decision for the First Minister alone and would not be included as part of the motion. However we suggest that such information might be made known to Members on an informal basis.

Junior Scottish Ministers

29.   The First Minister may, with the agreement of the Parliament, seek Her Majesty's approval to appoint junior Scottish Ministers. We propose that this should be handled in the same way as the appointment of Scottish Ministers.

Lord Advocate and Solicitor General

30.   The Scotland Act provides that the First Minister may recommend to Her Majesty the appointment or removal of a person as Lord Advocate or Solicitor General. The Parliament must first agree. We propose that the same procedure as that used for the appointment of Scottish Ministers should be used to secure the Parliament's agreement to the appointment of the Law Officers.

31.   A simple majority of those voting should be required to signify the Parliament's agreement to a Law Officer's removal.

Designation by the Presiding Officer

32.   The Scotland Act provides that if the office of First Minister is vacant or he or she is for any reason unable to act, the functions exercisable by the First Minister shall be exercisable by an MSP designated by the Presiding Officer.

33.   We recommend that the Standing Orders need prescribe only how the Presiding Officer's designation should be made and notified to the Parliament. We would expect the Presiding Officer to consult party leaders to identify a Member who would be accepted by the Parliament, but this is a matter best left to the Presiding Officer's discretion and to convention.

Vote of No Confidence in the Scottish Executive

34.   The First Minister must tender his or her resignation and Scottish Ministers, junior Scottish Ministers and Law Officers must resign if the Parliament resolves that the Scottish Executive no longer enjoys the confidence of the Parliament.   If the Parliament subsequently fails to nominate a successor First Minister then a general election has to be called. Given the significance of a vote of no confidence we consider that the procedures which should apply to such a vote should be carefully constructed.

35.   Any Member should be able to present a motion of no confidence in the Executive. This should be a debatable and amendable motion and should require a simple majority for approval. We recommend that if 26 or more MSPs sign a motion of no confidence, there should be an obligation on the Parliament to programme time for that motion to be debated and voted upon.

36.   The Parliament should also be able to consider a motion of no confidence in a named Minister. This is not a requirement of the Act and would not automatically lead to the resignation of the Minister concerned. However, if a Minister lost the confidence of the Parliament then the Minister and First Minister would need to consider whether the Minister should continue in office.

Resignations

37.   We recommend that Standing Orders should provide for the Presiding Officer to notify the Parliament of any resignations made by a member of the Scottish Executive.

Scottish Law Officers

Scotland Act

38.   Section 27 of the Scotland Act provides that if the Lord Advocate or the Solicitor General for Scotland is **not** a Member of the Parliament he or she may participate in the proceedings of the Parliament to the extent permitted by Standing Orders, but may not vote; and Standing Orders may in other respects provide that they are to apply to him or her as if he or she were a Member. By virtue of section 39(8)(b) the provisions of that section concerning Members' interests applies to the Lord Advocate and the Solicitor General as they apply to MSPs irrespective of whether the Lord Advocate and Solicitor General are themselves MSPs. These arrangements reflect the fact that as members of the Scottish Executive, the Law Officers should be accountable to the Parliament and should be able to be questioned (subject to the safeguards provided in the Scotland Act) on the performance of their Ministerial duties. Clearly should the Scottish Law Officers also be Members of the Parliament, they would be bound by the Parliament's Standing Orders.

General Principles

39.   We recommend that Standing Orders should be based around the general principle that, as members of the Scottish Executive, the Law Officers should be able to participate fully in Parliamentary proceedings, with the exception of being able to vote. Standing Orders should in all appropriate cases apply to them. By ensuring that Standing Orders remain flexible on this issue it is envisaged that the Parliament would develop its own conventions at a later date.

40.   In practical terms this means that the Law Officers should be able to participate in debates in the Plenary sessions like any Member of the Executive and to participate in adjournment type debates and to answer questions. They should be able to attend Committee sessions to the same extent as other members of the Executive; and should be able to steer through primary and secondary legislation for which they are the responsible Minister.

Members

Scotland Act

41.   Section 39 of the Scotland Act requires provision to be made, by or under an Act of the Scottish Parliament, for the registration and declaration of interests of Members of the Parliament and for restrictions on the participation of Members in the proceedings of the Parliament in certain circumstances where they have an interest in a matter to which the proceedings relate. In addition to this the Secretary of State invited CSG to consider and provide advice on the development of a Code of Conduct for MSPs.

Code of Conduct for MSPs

42.   We propose the following 9 key principles which should form the basis of a Code of Conduct for MSPs. They reflect the recommendations of the Nolan Committee on Standards in Public Life and are broadly consistent with the proposals for a Code of Ethics for Local Government in Scotland and the existing Code of Conduct for Westminster MPs.

Public Duty

Members have a duty to uphold the law and to act in accordance with the public trust placed in them; and a duty to act in the interests of the Scottish Parliament as a whole and the public it serves.

Duty to Constituents

Members have a duty to be accessible to their constituents. Members should consider carefully the views and wishes of their constituents; and, where appropriate, help ensure that constituents are able to pursue their concerns.

Selflessness

Members should take decisions solely in terms of the public interest. They should not do so in order to gain financial or other material benefits for themselves, their family or their friends.

Integrity

Members should not place themselves under any financial or other obligation to any individual or organisation that might influence them in the performance of their duties.

Honesty

Members have a duty to declare any private interests relating to their public duties and to take steps to resolve any conflicts arising in a way that protects the public interest.

Openness

Members should be as open as possible about all the decisions and actions they take. They should give reasons for their decisions and restrict information only when the wider public interest clearly demands. Where a Member has received information in confidence, or where disclosure of information might breach an individual's privacy, that confidence or privacy should be respected, unless there are overwhelming reasons in the wider public interest for disclosure to be made.

Responsibility for Decisions

Members remain responsible for any decision they take. In carrying out public business Members should consider issues on their merits taking account of the views of others.

Accountability

Members are accountable for their decisions and actions to the Scottish people and should submit themselves to whatever scrutiny is appropriate to their office.

Leadership

Members should promote and support these principles by leadership and example, to maintain and strengthen the public's trust and confidence in the integrity of Members in conducting public business.

Arrangements for Taking the Oath

43. Under the provisions of the Scotland Act MSPs will be required to take the oath of allegiance provided by the Promissory Oaths Act 1868 or to make the corresponding affirmation. If they do not do so within 2 months of the day they are returned, or such longer period as the Parliament may allow then they shall cease to be a Member and their seat will become vacant. No payment of salary or allowances may be made to a Member until the oath is taken. Nor may they participate in the proceedings of the Parliament until they have done so.

44. We propose that the Standing Orders for the Scottish Parliament should prescribe that the Clerk should officiate over the taking of oaths prior to the election of the Presiding Officer.

45. The Scotland Act provides that the oaths must be taken in meetings of the Parliament. It is proposed that this should be the first business of the new Parliament, prior to election of the Presiding Officer.

46. Only the version of the oath as it is set out in the legislation is legally acceptable. We recommend that Members should be able to repeat the oath in a language other than English.

Notifying the Presiding Officer of Resignation

47. Section 14 of the Scotland Act provides that an MSP may at any time resign his or her seat by giving notice in writing to the Presiding Officer.

48. It is proposed that the Standing Orders should provide for this to be notified to the Parliament by being lodged with the Clerk by the Presiding Officer and published.

Determination of a Vacancy

49. Sections 9(5) and 10(7) of the Scotland Act provide for the date on which a constituency vacancy and a regional vacancy occur respectively to be determined under Standing Orders. A by-election must be held within 3 months of a constituency seat becoming vacant. There is no time limit for filling a regional vacancy since that will normally be filled by the next person on the list, or left vacant if originally filled by an independent candidate.

50. Constituency vacancies can occur in a number of ways. For example in the event of a death, we suggest that the date should be the date on which the death occurred. In the event of resignation, it might be the date on which the resignation was notified to the Parliament by the Presiding Officer. There will be other ways in which a vacancy may occur. We propose that Standing Orders should simply provide that the date is determined as being the date which is announced to the Parliament by the Presiding Officer, or certified by the Presiding Officer, thus moving the discretion on to the Presiding Officer.

Scottish Parliamentary Corporate Body

Scotland Act

51.   Section 21 of the Scotland Act states that there shall be a Scottish Parliamentary Corporate Body (SPCB) "to perform the functions conferred on the corporation by virtue of this Act or any other enactment". It also states that the five members of this corporate body will be the Presiding Officer and "four members of the Parliament appointed in accordance with standing orders".

Appointment of MSPs

52.   We suggest that the four members of the SPCB should be elected by ballot. Nominations should be sought from the Plenary, and nominees should be supported by one proposer and one seconder. The election process would be similar to that for the election of the Presiding Officer and Deputies.

Party issues

53.   We recommend that Standing Orders make no prescription in respect of ensuring that the four members of the SPCB come from different political parties. The appointment of members to the SPCB is not a political one, and members will still enjoy full voting rights within the Parliament. Indeed, there would be nothing to prevent an independent Member from becoming a member of the SPCB. MSPs' choice should not be restricted, although they may wish to appoint SPCB members from across the political spectrum and indeed we expect all parties will want to contribute to the administration of the Parliament. We believe that a broad provision for the election of Members to the SPCB is all that is needed in Standing Orders.

Time limits

54.   The Scotland Act does not prescribe any time limit within which the Parliament must elect Members to the SPCB. The SPCB will, however, be responsible for a number of important functions and it would be imprudent for its positions to remain vacant for longer than is necessary. We recommend that if the Scottish Parliament has been unable to appoint 4 Members within, say, one month of the election, the Presiding Officer should be given the power to make appointment of Members to the SPCB.

Resignations/Removal/Further elections

55.   Paragraph 1 of Schedule 2 of the Scotland Act contemplates that a member of the SPCB will cease to hold office if either he or she resigns or ceases to be a Member of the Parliament otherwise than by virtue of a dissolution, or if another Member of the Parliament is appointed in his or her place. Standing Orders should therefore make provisions about the circumstances in which there should be the appointment of a new member of the SPCB to replace a sitting member. We recommend that Standing Orders are flexible rather than prescriptive on this point to allow the Scottish Parliament to elect a new member whenever the Parliament wants, and where necessary to allow the Presiding Officer to appoint.

56.   Any member of the SPCB would be free to resign at any time. Resignations would be intimated to the Presiding Officer, who would announce the resignation to Parliament and ensure that it was published.

57.   We recommend that new appointments to the SPCB should take place after each General Election to the Parliament. This would allow the Parliament to make its own endorsements.

Committees of the Parliament

58.   In section 2, we set out our proposals for all-purpose subject Committees, which would combine the role of the Westminster Standing and Select Committee, with the following functions:

- to consider and report on the policy and administration of the Scottish Administration;

- to conduct inquiries into such matters or issues as the Parliament may require;

- to scrutinise primary and secondary legislation and proposed European Union legislation;

- to initiate legislation;

- to scrutinise financial proposals and administration of the Scottish Executive (including variation of taxes, estimates, appropriation and audit); and

- to scrutinise procedures relating to the Parliament and its Members (including adherence to those procedures).

59.   In all cases the Committees should report to the Parliament with recommendations.

60.   While we have taken the general view that it should be for the Parliament, once established, to make the final decision on its Committee structure and the remit of those Committees, we concluded, however, that there are certain Committees whose functions are so fundamental to the running of the Parliament that these should be required to be established. These Committees are:

- a Business Committee;

- a Procedures Committee;

- a Standards Committee;

- an Audit Committee;

- a Finance Committee;

- a European Committee;

- an Equal Opportunities Committee;

- a Public Petitions Committee;

- a Delegated Legislation Committee.

Business Committee

61.   We recommend that Standing Orders should provide for a Business Committee to be established as soon as possible after each General Election to the Scottish Parliament.

62.   The functions of the Business Committee should be:

- to prepare the programme of Business of the Parliament;

- to timetable the daily order of Business for the Plenary session;

- to timetable the progress of legislation in Committees;

- to propose the remit, membership, duration and budget of Parliamentary Committees; and

- any other tasks (other than SPCB functions) related to the conduct of the Parliament's business which the Parliament may ask it to perform.

63.   The members of the Business Committee should be: the Presiding Officer (as Convener of the Business Committee) and a Member nominated by the leader of each party with 5 or more Members elected to the Parliament. We expect that each party will want to be represented by its Business Manager. Independents and smaller parties should be able to gain representation on the Business Committee if they group together to form a group with 5 or more Members. Such a grouping should be able to nominate a representative to sit on the Business Committee.

64.   The two Deputy Presiding Officers, and the Chair of the Committee of Conveners, should one be established, should be entitled to attend meetings of the Business Committee but not to vote. The only exception to this should be where the Presiding Officer was temporarily unable to exercise his or her functions as Convener of the Business Committee. In such a situation, a Deputy Presiding Officer should act in the capacity of Convener.

65.   There should be no quorum for the Business Committee. Members of the Business Committee unable to attend a meeting of the Committee should be entitled to send a substitute in their place.

66.   Should the Business Committee require to vote on any issue within its remit, voting should be weighted to reflect the number of Members in the Parliament which each participant on the Committee represents. The Presiding Officer, or his or her Deputy if in the chair, should have only a casting vote in the event of a tie.

67.   It should be the responsibility of the Business Committee to determine the forward programme of business, except for that Parliamentary business which is elsewhere determined in Standing Orders.

68.   The Business Committee should put a regular programme of business to the Parliament for the Parliament to approve. It should agree the timetable for the consideration of legislation in Committees (subject to any provisions elsewhere in Standing Orders about timing of stages of Bills). It should also agree an overall timetable for the consideration of other business in the Committees, including the conduct of inquiries. Parliamentary

Committees should be able to programme their own business within the timescale agreed by the Parliament on the proposal of the Business Committee.

69.   The Business motion should be debatable but the debate on it should be time limited to 30 minutes. Members should be able to table amendments to the Business Programme, provided at least 10 MSPs subscribe to the amendment. Debate on any single amendment should be limited to one speaker for, and one speaker against, each speaking for no more than 3 minutes. The Executive's representative on the Business Committee would be expected to speak for the Business motion.

70.   The Business Committee should also plan the daily timetable of business in the Plenary, including the timetabling of debates on Bills.

71.   The Business Committee should make recommendations to the Parliament for the establishment, terms of reference, budget, membership and duration of Committees of the Parliament.

72.   In making recommendations on membership the Business Committee should take into account the expertise of Members, any preferences expressed by Members, the requirements of the Scotland Act (eg as to the balance of parties) and of the law generally (eg regarding equal opportunities).

73.   It should be open to any Member to propose the establishment of a Committee: the Business Committee should consider any such proposals and report with recommendations to the Parliament.

74.   Business Committee recommendations on the establishment of Committees and sub-Committees should require the approval of the Parliament.

Standards Committee

75.   A Standards Committee with a membership of 5 to 15 should be established for the duration of the Parliament.

76.   The remit of the Standards Committee will be informed by the report from Code of Conduct Working Group.

Procedures Committee

77.   A Procedures Committee with a membership of 5 to 15 should be established for the duration of the Parliament.

78.   The remit of the Procedures Committee should be to consider the practice and procedures of the Parliament in relation to its public business, to monitor, review and advise upon the Parliament's Standing Orders, to monitor the Parliament's performance in applying the CSG key principles and to make recommendations.

Audit Committee

79.   The Parliament should establish an Audit Committee with a membership of 5 to 15 for the duration of the Parliament.

80.   The remit of the Audit Committee should be to consider financial audit reports commissioned by the Auditor General for Scotland. The Audit Committee will also monitor matters of regularity and propriety within the Parliament and Executive. In addition, the Audit Committee may, separately or in conjunction with the relevant subject Committee when this is appropriate, consider the findings of value for money studies commissioned by the Auditor General for Scotland.

Finance Committee

81.   The Parliament should establish a Finance Committee with a membership of 5 to 15 for the duration of the Parliament.

82.   The remit of the Finance Committee should be to comment on reports on financial issues provided by the subject Committees and, having given due consideration to the financial performance of the Executive, scrutinise the Executive's budget proposals. The Committee may also consider issues relating to the Executive's budgetary policy, as well as performance monitoring issues relating to wide ranging financial matters such as the assigned budget and the annual financial report. The Finance Committee will also support the Business Committee in co-ordinating the progress of financial legislation.

European Committee

83.   The Parliament should establish a European Committee for the duration of the Parliament.

84.   The remit of the European Committee should be: to sift relevant EU-related documents on behalf of the Parliament, and to take further action as necessary, whether through further consideration of the documents within the European Committee or through referral to the relevant subject Committee or to the Plenary; and to debate wider EU topics.

85.   It should have between 5 and 15 members, recommended by the Business Committee. In recommending members to the European Committee, the Business Committee should recommend members already recommended to other Committees whose work is considered relevant to that of the European Committee, although not to the exclusion of those not so recommended.

86.   The Convener of the European Committee should not be a Convener of another Committee considered relevant to the European Committee.

Equal Opportunities Committee

87.   The Parliament should establish an Equal Opportunities Committee with a membership of 5 to 15 for the duration of the Parliament.

88.   The remit of the Equal Opportunities Committee will be to develop equal opportunities policies for the Parliament and to monitor the delivery of equal opportunities within the policy making of the Parliament with the aim of ensuring mainstreaming of equal opportunities.

Public Petitions Committee

89.   The Parliament should establish a Public Petitions Committee with a membership of 5 to 15 for the duration of the Parliament.

90.   The remit of the Public Petitions Committee should be to decide whether the remedy sought by the petitioner falls within the competence of the Parliament; to acknowledge receipt of all petitions within 5 sitting days and to inform petitioners of the action and decisions the Committee had taken within 42 sitting days.

Delegated Legislation Committee

91.   The Parliament should establish a Delegated Legislation Committee with a membership of 5 to 15 for the duration of the Parliament.

92.   Its remit should be: to examine the provisions within Bills conferring powers to make subordinate legislation and to report; and to examine subordinate legislation brought before the Parliament to assess whether it is *intra-vires*. The Committee should be able to report its concerns on any technical aspect of subordinate legislation.

General Membership of Committees and Sub-Committees

93.   Paragraph 71 above sets out our proposals for the role of the Business Committee in making recommendations for the establishment and membership of general all purpose Committees as described in paragraph 12 of section 2. The Business Committee should also consider requests from MSPs or Committees for a particular Committee to be disbanded. Recommendations on such disbandment should be put to the Parliament for its approval. The Business Committee should be able to put such a recommendation to the Parliament, without a request from an MSP or Committee.

94.   Committees should have the right to establish sub-Committees. Membership of sub-Committees shall be approved by the relevant Committee. Proposals for the establishment and remit of sub-Committees should be approved by the Business Committee, and approved by the Parliament in the same way as establishment of Committees.

95.   Only MSPs may be full voting members of Committees. Any MSP may put him/herself forward for consideration as a member of a Committee (other than the Business Committee) by submitting a formal indication of interest to the Business Committee.

96.   Each Committee should have between 5 and 15 members.

97.   In making recommendations on Committee membership to the Plenary, the Business Committee must have due regard to the balance of parties within the Parliament. Selection of members must not be on the basis of random selection.

98.   The Business Committee, having due regard to the balance of parties within the Parliament, should propose the political party from which a Committee's Convener should be elected. The Committee's members would then elect their Convener subject to that limitation.

99.   Should an MSP who is a member of a Committee no longer be able or wish to fulfil

that role, the Business Committee should recommend a replacement member, again having due regard to the balance of parties within the Parliament.

100. Should the Committee Convener no longer be able to fulfil his or her role, the Committee should elect a new Convener from the same party. If there is no other representative of that political group on the Committee, the Business Committee should indicate the party or political grouping from which a new Committee Convener should be chosen, having due regard to the balance of parties within the Parliament.

Quorums

101. A quorum of 3 Members must be reached by Committees both for consideration of business **and** for voting. Only MSPs should be counted in respect of the calculation of a quorum. Committees which are not quorate should not be able to meet. The only exception to this is the Business Committee, proposals for which are detailed below.

Witnesses and Documents

102. Standing Orders should authorise all Committees of the Parliament to exercise the power provided in section 23 of the Scotland Act to call for witnesses and documents.

Reporters

103. Committees should have the right to appoint from their members, should they wish, a reporter in whose name a report would be submitted to the Plenary. This should be a broad provision which would encourage but not oblige Committees to appoint reporters. It is not proposed that Standing Orders should prescribe the potential functions which a reporter might adopt within the Committee, as this should be dependent on the wishes of a particular Committee.

Power of Summons

104. Sections 23 to 26 of the Scotland Act give the Parliament the power, subject to certain conditions and exclusions, to require persons to attend its proceedings to give evidence, or to produce documents.

105. It is anticipated that witnesses and documents will usually be invited rather than summoned to attend proceedings. In general, the Parliament should summon witnesses with a reasonable period of notice, because to do otherwise might provide witnesses or those providing documents with what the courts could interpret as a "reasonable excuse" not to comply. However, matters will depend on the circumstances of each case and there could be cases where a very short period of notice is appropriate.

106. It is proposed that Standing Orders should not therefore provide for a minimum notice period, but leave as much flexibility as possible to the Parliament.

Oath

107. Section 26 of the Scotland Act provides that the Presiding Officer, or other person authorised by Standing Orders, may administer an oath or require that a person attending take an oath or affirmation.

108. As most witnesses will be appearing in front of Committees, Standing Orders should provide for Committee Conveners to require that an oath be taken, and for the oath to be administered by the Clerk to the Committee in such circumstances.

Travel and Subsistence

109. Section 26, subsection (4) of the Scotland Act allows Standing Orders to provide for the payment of allowances and expenses to those giving evidence or producing documents to the Parliament.

110. We propose that Standing Orders should make provision for such payment to be made, but that the SPCB should be left to decide the specific administrative arrangements and the amounts to be paid.

Participation of Ministers in Committee proceedings

111. While it would not be appropriate for Ministers to participate in Committee proceedings which involve scrutinising the Executive, there should be a role for Ministers in Committee work which involves the consideration of legislation, either primary or secondary, as the presence of a Minister during the discussion would be invaluable in indicating the intentions of the Executive and the likelihood of suggested amendments being acceptable to the Government. At the same time, the Parliament, through its Committees, will want the Government to explain its proposed legislation. Standing Orders should set down which Committee functions should be undertaken with a contribution from Ministers.

112. Standing Orders should provide for the Minister responsible for a particular piece of legislation (or his or her representative) to participate in the work of a Committee when that Committee is scrutinising that legislation (whether it be primary, secondary or draft European legislation). The Minister should not have voting rights on the Committee.

113. The same provision should be extended to any other Member who is responsible for a piece of legislation before the Committee (eg on a Private Member's Bill). Again any MSP should have the right to attend Committee proceedings, unless they are excluded following a motion passed in Plenary. Non-members of Committees should have no voting rights, and should not count towards the calculation of a quorum.

Location of Committees

114. We recommend that, once the remits of the Committees of the Scottish Parliament have been agreed, the Parliament should identify a number of Committees which should be permanently based in a location other than Edinburgh. The location should be relevant to the remit of the particular Committee, taking into account the location of the people most affected by the decisions of the Committee, and the objective of spreading the location of some Committees geographically around Scotland. All subject Committees should be encouraged to meet around Scotland.

Budgets

115. Committees' budgets should be allocated at the start of each financial year with the agreement of the Parliament on the recommendation of the Business Committee, which

would thereafter be responsible for the monitoring of Committees' expenditure. Should a Committee wish to exceed their budget they should be required by Standing Orders to seek the Business Committee's approval. Should the Business Committee decide not to approve the Committee's proposal then it should be open to the Committee to put the matter to a vote of the whole House via a motion that should be both debatable and amendable. In addition, should Members need to travel overseas on business related to the Parliament, then they should be required to give the Business Committee prior notification.

Summary of Recommendations for Standing Orders

Standing Orders should provide that:

Presiding Officer

- when there is no Presiding Officer, the oldest Member in the Parliament, who is not a candidate for the posts of Presiding Officer, Deputy Presiding Officer or First Minister, should preside over the election of the Presiding Officer or Deputy.

- during the first stage of the election of the Presiding Officer, nominations, which should be seconded, should be made from the Plenary. A set period should be allowed for such nominations to be made. A successful candidate should be given the opportunity to speak to accept election after the vote.

- nominations should be able to be made only at the beginning of the process, not between successive votes.

- a ballot should be held, overseen by the Clerk and 2 scrutineers drawn by lots from the members who are not candidates.

- if there are more than 2 candidates, the candidate receiving the fewest number of votes in the first ballot should drop out, and successive ballots should be held until a clear winning candidate has been identified.

- the winning candidate should command the support of a simple majority of Members voting, subject to a quorum for the number of Members voting of 25% of all the seats in the Parliament.

- if a clear winner is not identified, the process should begin afresh.

- the DPOs should be elected successively after the Presiding Officer. If the Presiding Officer and first Deputy Presiding Officer elected came from the same political party, then nominations for the second Deputy Presiding Officer should not be allowed for candidates from that party.

- the Presiding Officer should have only a casting vote in the proceedings of the Parliament.

- there should be no restriction on the DPOs' powers to participate in debate or to vote unless they are presiding over the business of the Parliament at the time, when they should have only a casting vote.

- the Presiding Officer and the Deputies may resign at any time. The Deputy

Presiding Officers should intimate resignation to the Presiding Officer, who should announce the resignation to Parliament. The Presiding Officer should announce his/her resignation to Parliament. Resignations should be published.

- there should be a maximum period of 14 sitting days between the resignation of a Presiding Officer or Deputy Presiding Officer and the holding of an election for a successor.

- the Presiding Officer may be removed from office only by an absolute majority of the number of seats in the Parliament: ie, at least 65 votes in favour of removal would be required. The same should apply to Deputy Presiding Officers.

- the Presiding Officer should be able to delegate any of his/her functions to the Deputy Presiding Officers, subject to the provisions of the Scotland Act.

Scottish Executive

- the appointment of the First Minister should have 3 main stages:

    - nomination of a candidate by the Parliament;

    - recommendation of the nominated candidate by the Presiding Officer to Her Majesty for appointment;

    - appointment of the First Minister by Her Majesty.

- any MSP, provided they are supported by a proposer and a seconder, should be able to stand for nomination for First Minister. The names of candidates should be submitted to the Presiding Officer. Following this an election or series of elections should take place by means of a roll call vote of MSPs, in which names should be progressively eliminated until one candidate emerged who enjoyed the support of a simple majority of MSPs. A quorum for voting, subject to 25% of the total number of seats, would be required. The successful candidate should then be recommended by the Presiding Officer to Her Majesty the Queen for appointment.

- the same procedure as for the appointment of Scottish Ministers should be used for the appointment of Junior Ministers and Law Officers.

- a simple majority of those voting should be required to signify the Parliament's agreement to a Law Officer's removal.

- any Member should be able to present a motion of no confidence in the Executive. This would be a debatable and amendable motion and would require a simple majority for approval. If 26 or more MSPs sign a motion of no confidence, there should be an obligation on the Parliament to programme time for that motion to be debated and voted upon.

- the Parliament should also be able to consider a motion of no confidence in a named Minister.

- the Presiding Officer should notify the Parliament of any resignations made by Members of the Scottish Executive.

- Law Officers should be subject to Standing Orders in all relevant cases where they apply to them.

Oaths

- the Clerk should officiate over the taking of oaths as the first business after an election prior to the election of the Presiding Officer.

Resignations

- resignations by MSPs should be notified to the Parliament by being lodged with the Clerk by the Presiding Officer and by being published.

Vacancies

- the date of a constituency vacancy should be determined as being the date which is announced to the Parliament by the Presiding Officer or certified by the Presiding Officer.

SPCB

- the 4 members of the SPCB should be elected by ballot. Nominations should be sought from the Plenary, and nominees should be supported by one proposer and one seconder. The election process should be similar to that for the election of the Presiding Officer and Deputies.

- the Parliament should be able to elect a new member to the SPCB when it wants, and the Presiding Officer should also be able to appoint members to the SPCB.

- resignations of members of the SPCB should be intimated to the Presiding Officer, who should announce the resignation to Parliament and ensure that it is published.

- new appointments to the SPCB should take place after each General Election.

Committees

All-purpose Subject Committees

- the Parliament should be able to establish Committees able to:

  - consider and report on the policy and administration of the Scottish Administration;

  - conduct inquiries into such matters or issues as the Parliament may require;

  - scrutinise primary and secondary legislation and proposed European Union legislation;

- initiate legislation;

- scrutinise financial proposals and administration of the Scottish Executive (including variation of taxes, estimates, appropriation and audit); and

- scrutinise procedures relating to the Parliament and its Members (including adherence to those procedures).

- in all cases, Committees should report to the Parliament with recommendations.

Business Committee

- Standing Orders should provide for a Business Committee to be established as soon as possible after each General Election to the Scottish Parliament.

- the functions of the Business Committee should be:

  - to prepare the programme of Business of the Parliament;

  - to timetable the daily order of Business for the Plenary session;

  - to timetable the progress of legislation in Committees;

  - to propose the remit, membership, duration and budget of Parliamentary Committees; and

  - any other tasks (other than SPCB functions) related to the conduct of the Parliament's business which the Parliament may ask it to perform.

- the members of the Business Committee should be: the Presiding Officer (as Chair of the Business Committee) and a member nominated by the leader of each party with 5 or more Members elected to the Parliament. Independents and smaller parties should be able to be represented on the Business Committee if they group together to form a group with 5 or more Members. Such a grouping should be able to nominate a representative to sit on the Business Committee.

- the two Deputy Presiding Officers, and the Chairman of the Committee of Conveners, should one be established, should be entitled to attend meetings of the Business Committee but not to vote. The only exception to this would be where the Presiding Officer was temporarily unable to exercise his or her functions as Convener of the Business Committee. In such a situation, a Deputy Presiding Officer should act in the capacity of Convener.

- there should be no quorum for the Business Committee. Members of the Business Committee unable to attend a meeting of the Committee should be entitled to send a substitute in their place.

- should the Business Committee require to vote on any issue within its remit, voting should be weighted to reflect the number of members in the Parliament which each participant on the Committee represents. The Presiding Officer, or his or her Deputy if in the Chair, should have a casting vote only in the event of a tie.

- the Business motion should be debatable but the debate on it should be time limited to 30 minutes. Members should be able to table amendments to the Business Programme, provided at least 10 MSPs subscribe to the amendment. Debate on any single amendment should be limited to one speaker for, and one speaker against, each speaking for no more than 3 minutes. The Executive's representative on the Business Committee should be expected to speak for the Business motion.

- the Business Committee should make recommendations to the Parliament for the establishment, terms of reference, budget, membership and duration of Committees of the Parliament.

- it should be open to any member to propose the establishment of a Committee: the Business Committee should consider any such proposals and report with recommendations to the Parliament.

Standards Committee

- a Standards Committee with a membership of 5 to 15 should be established for the duration of the Parliament.

Procedures Committee

- a Procedures Committee with a membership of 5 to 15 should be established for the duration of the Parliament.

- the remit of the Procedures Committee should be: to consider the practice and procedures of the Parliament in relation to its public business, to monitor and review the Parliament's Standing Orders, to monitor the Parliament's performance in applying the CSG key principles and to make recommendations.

Audit Committee

- the Parliament should establish an Audit Committee with a membership of 5 to 15 for the duration of the Parliament.

- the remit of the Audit Committee should be to consider financial audit reports commissioned by the Auditor General for Scotland. The Audit Committee will also monitor matters of regularity and propriety within the Parliament and Executive. In addition, the Audit Committee may, separately or in conjunction with the relevant subject Committee when this is appropriate, consider the findings of value for money studies commissioned by the Auditor General for Scotland.

Finance Committee

- the Parliament should establish a Finance Committee with a membership of 5 to 15 for the duration of the Parliament.

- the remit of the Finance Committee should be to comment on reports on financial issues provided by the subject Committees and, having given due consideration to the financial performance of the Executive, scrutinise the Executive's budget proposals. The Committee may also consider issues relating to the Executive's budgetary policy, as well as performance monitoring issues relating to wide ranging financial matters such as the assigned budget and the annual financial report. The Finance Committee will also support the Business Committee in co-ordinating the progress of financial legislation.

European Committee

- the Parliament should establish a European Committee for the duration of the Parliament.

- the remit of the European Committee should be: to sift relevant EU-related documents on behalf of the Parliament, and to take further action as necessary, whether through further consideration of the documents within the European Committee or through referral to the relevant subject Committee or to the Plenary; and to debate wider EU topics.

- it should have between 5 and 15 members, recommended by the Business Committee. In recommending members to the European Committee, the Business Committee should recommend members already recommended to other Committees whose work is considered relevant to that of the European Committee, although not to the exclusion of those not so recommended.

- the Convener of the European Committee should not be a Convener of another Committee considered relevant to the European Committee.

Equal Opportunities Committee

- the Parliament should establish an Equal Opportunities Committee with a membership of 5 to 15 for the duration of the Parliament.

- the remit of the Equal Opportunities Committee should be to develop equal opportunities policies for the Parliament and to monitor the delivery of equal opportunities within the policy making of the Parliament with the aim of ensuring mainstreaming of equal opportunities.

Public Petitions Committee

- the Parliament should establish a Public Petitions Committee with a membership of 5 to 15 for the duration of the Parliament.

- the remit of the Public Petitions Committee should be: to decide whether the remedy sought by the petitioner falls within the competence of the Parliament; to acknowledge receipt of all petitions within 5 sitting days and to inform petitioners of the action and decisions the Committee had taken within 42 sitting days.

Delegated Legislation Committee

- the Parliament should establish a Delegated Legislation Committee with a membership of 5 to 15 for the duration of the Parliament.

- its remit should be: to examine the provisions within Bills conferring powers to make subordinate legislation and to report; and to examine subordinate legislation brought before the Parliament to assess whether it is *intra-vires*. The Committee should be able to report its concerns on any technical aspect of subordinate legislation.

General: Membership of Committees and Sub-Committees

- Committees should have the right to establish sub-Committees. Membership of sub-Committees shall be approved by the relevant Committee. Proposals for the establishment and remit of sub-Committees should be approved by the Business Committee, and approved by Parliament in the same way as establishment of Committees.

- only MSPs should be able to be full voting members of Committees.

- each Committee should have between 5 and 15 members.

- in making recommendations on Committee membership to the Plenary, the Business Committee must have due regard to the balance of parties within the Parliament.

- the Business Committee, having due regard to the balance of parties within the Parliament, should propose the political party from which a Committee's Convener should be elected. The Committee's members should elect their Convener subject to that limitation.

- should an MSP who is a member of a Committee no longer be able or wish to fulfil that role, the Business Committee should recommend a replacement member, again having due regard to the balance of parties within the Parliament.

- should the Committee Convener no longer be able to fulfil his or her role, the Committee should elect a new Convener from the same party. If there is no other representative of that party or political group on the Committee, the Business Committee should indicate the party or political grouping from which a new Committee Convener should be chosen, having due regard to the balance of parties within the Parliament.

Quorums

- a quorum of 3 must be reached by Committees both for consideration of business and for voting. Only MSPs should be counted in respect of the calculation of a quorum. Committees which are not quorate should not be able to meet.

Witnesses and Documents

- Standing Orders should authorise all Committees of the Parliament to exercise the power provided in section 23 of the Scotland Act to call for witnesses and documents.

Reporters

- Committees should have the right to appoint from their members, should they wish, a reporter.

Allowances

- provision should be made for the payment of allowances and expenses to those giving evidence or producing documents to the Parliament.

Non-Committee Members

- Standing Orders should set down which Committee functions should be undertaken with a contribution from Ministers.

- Standing Orders should provide for the Minister responsible for a particular piece of legislation (or his or her representative) to participate in the work of a Committee when that Committee is scrutinising that legislation (whether it be primary, secondary or draft European legislation). The Minister should not have voting rights on the Committee.

- the same provision should be extended to any other Member who is responsible for a piece of legislation before the Committee (eg on a Private Member's Bill). Again any MSP should have the right to attend Committee proceedings, unless they are excluded following a motion passed in Plenary.

Location

- provision should be made for Committees to be based outside Edinburgh, and for Committees to travel.

Budgets

- Committees' budgets should be allocated at the start of each financial year with the agreement of the Parliament on the recommendation of the Business Committee, which would thereafter be responsible for the monitoring of Committees' expenditure. Should a Committee wish to exceed their budget they should be required by Standing Orders to seek the Business Committee's approval. Should the Business Committee decide not to approve the Committee's proposal then it should be open to the Committee to put the matter to a vote of the Plenary via a motion that should be both debatable and amendable. In addition, should Members need to travel overseas on business related to the

Parliament, then they should be required to give the Business Committee prior notification.

Powers

- Committees should have the power to conduct joint meetings and inquiries.

- Committees should be able to establish one or more expert panels, of varying duration. Rules governing appointments to such Committees should ensure that appointments are made on merit and reflect a comprehensive range of opinion and expertise.

- Committees should be able to co-opt non-MSPs as non-voting members. Rules governing appointments should ensure that such appointments are made on merit.

SECTION 3.3:

PARLIAMENTARY BUSINESS

1. This section sets out our recommendations on the programming of business in the Parliament, the sitting pattern of the Parliament, the conduct of Parliamentary business, the reporting of proceedings and related issues. In considering these issues we have been guided by the principle that power should be shared in the Parliament, and that the interests of non-Executive parties and individual members should be protected; the principle of openness and accessibility, reflected in our desire to deliver procedures which are modern, accessible and relevant; together with the principles of accountability and equal opportunities.

Programming of Business

2. Consistent with our key principle of openness and accessibility, we recommend that the Parliament should seek to operate open and transparent systems for planning and timetabling business. The sitting pattern of the Parliament including the allocation of time for Committee, Plenary and for party political and constituency business, together with details of planned Summer, October, Christmas and Easter recesses, should be publicised at the beginning of each Parliamentary year (recognising that this might need to be changed, in the light of unforeseen developments).

3. We propose that the Business Committee should put a regular programme of business to the Parliament for the Parliament to approve. This might be done on a weekly basis looking at the forthcoming two weeks. The Business motion should be debatable but the debate on it should be time limited. We recommend that Members should be able to table amendments to the Business Programme, provided a minimum number of MSPs, say 10, subscribe to the amendment.

4. The Business Committee as well as recommending a forward programme for business in the Plenary, should agree the timetable for the consideration of legislation in Committees (subject to any provisions in Standing Orders about timing of stages of Bills). It should also agree an overall timetable for the consideration of other business in the Committees, including the conduct of inquiries. Parliamentary Committees should be able to programme their own business within the timescale agreed by the Parliament on the proposal of the Business Committee.

5. The Business Committee should also plan the daily timetable of Business in the Plenary, including the timetabling of debates on Bills. This would provide an agreed approach to the handling of debates and legislation aimed at ensuring that Members had sufficient time to focus on areas of interest to them, balanced against the need to conduct the business of the Parliament efficiently.

6. Some Parliamentary business is likely to be prescribed by Standing Orders eg the periods to be devoted to Questions to Ministers. Standing Orders should at least prescribe a minimum amount of time for matters such as Committee and other non-Executive business.

Private Members' business

7. We recommend that time should be set aside after the votes at the end of the day specifically for private members' business. This would allow members to raise non-controversial, constituency-related issues. Members should also be able to table motions for publication on the order paper. It will be for the Business Committee to make recommendations to the Parliament on which motions should be debated and voted upon.

8. In the case of legislation initiated by Private Members, it is suggested that it be left to the Business Committee to allocate time to Bills which are to be introduced. It is thought that the approval of the Scottish Parliament itself (which will already have been secured) for the Bill to be given time should be sufficient to drive that process.

Committees

9. Standing Orders should prescribe a minimum amount of Parliamentary time when Committee business eg the discussion of Committee reports and the introduction of Committee-initiated legislation approved by the Parliament, should be given precedence over the business of the Executive. One option would be for Standing Orders to specify a weekly/monthly period of time for such business; alternatively Standing Orders could provide for a minimum period of Parliamentary time to be distributed at the discretion of the Business Committee.

Non-Executive Parties

10. It might be helpful at the outset to provide some framework or guidance for the Business Committee in allocating time to non-Executive party business. Once the Scottish Parliament has been operating for some time, the Parliament would be able to take a view on the necessity of such a provision. We propose that Standing Orders prescribe a minimum amount of time for such business, say 12 days per year. The division of this time could be done on the basis of the balance of the parties in the Parliament.

11. There are other categories of business where it might be considered more appropriate for Standing Orders to give the Presiding Officer a role in the allocation of Parliamentary time, eg in consideration of a request from a member to debate a matter of urgent public importance in Plenary session and it is proposed that the Presiding Officer should be given such discretion.

Sitting Periods

12. In keeping with the concept of a family-friendly Parliament, the Parliament should be in session for approximately 30-33 weeks per year. This would allow an 8-10 week break in summer from mid-June until end-August and with 2-4 week breaks at Easter and Christmas. Additional mid-term breaks in February and October could also be built in. The sitting pattern of the Parliament including the allocation of time for Committee, Plenary and for party political activities should be agreed and publicised at the beginning of each Parliamentary year (recognising that it would be possible for this to change, based on the requirements of the Parliament).

13. Committees should not sit when the Plenary is in session, to facilitate maximum participation in debates. We also believe that time for party business should be built in to

avoid the possibility of party business encroaching into non-Parliamentary time, ie evenings and weekends.

14. A possible model for the sitting pattern of the Scottish Parliament might be:

Monday am   - Travelling and constituency business
Monday pm   - Additional Committee/Plenary business and party political
                                     activity
Tuesday 9.30am-12.30pm   - Committee
Tuesday 12.30pm-2.30pm   - Lunch/time for party political and constituency activities
Tuesday 2.30pm-5.30pm   - Committee
Wednesday 9.30am-12.30pm - Committee
Wednesday 12.30pm-2.30pm - Lunch/time for party political and constituency activities
Wednesday 2.30pm-5.30pm - Plenary
Thursday 9.30am-12.30pm   - Plenary
Thursday 12.30pm-2.30pm   - Lunch/time for party political and constituency activities
Thursday 2.30pm-5.30pm   - Plenary
Friday am/pm   - Additional Committee/Plenary business and party political
                                     activity

Location of Plenary Sessions

15. Section 2 of the Scotland Act provides for the Secretary of State to designate the location of the **first** meeting of the new Scottish Parliament. We recommend that Standing Orders should provide for the Presiding Officer to determine the Parliament's meeting place thereafter. This is expected to be in Edinburgh, but such a provision would give the Parliament the flexibility to meet elsewhere if required.

Location of Committee Sessions

16. Explicit provision designating the location of Committee meetings would not be appropriate. We propose that Standing Orders should include provision enabling Committees to meet anywhere within Scotland.

Sitting Days/Hours: Provision in Standing Orders

17. Given our proposals for a Business Committee which would be responsible for the detailed planning and timetabling of the Parliament's business, it is proposed that only general provisions relating to the sitting times are included in Standing Orders, for example, Standing Orders might prescribe that:

- the Parliament should normally meet between the hours of 9.30am and 5.30pm on Tuesday to Thursday; 2.30pm to 5.30pm on Monday; 9.30am to 12.30pm on Friday;

- the Parliament should be in Recess for a specified number of weeks per year which would enable it to break for the Scottish school holidays; and

- Committees should be able to meet at other times when the Plenary itself is not in session.

Voting Times

18.   We recommend that where possible voting in the Parliament should take place at a regular appointed time, for example towards the end of the day on the day's business, say from 5pm onwards for Plenary sessions or at the end of a Committee session.

19.   It is important to schedule votes for the same day as the associated discussion to ensure that debates are fresh in Members' minds. The scheduling of votes at a set time each day, as proposed above, would ensure the most effective use of Parliamentary and MSPs' time. Such an arrangement would also allow Parliamentary and Members' staff to plan other business around this time.

20.   We considered whether scheduling the voting in this way would be appropriate for all types of Parliamentary Business. We concluded that it would be necessary to allow sequential votes on amendments to legislation, as debate on a particular clause could be coloured by a decision to amend a previous clause. An exception should therefore be made for consideration of legislation. Voting on nominations for the Presiding Officer, First Minister etc, should also be held at the appropriate point in the day. We also recommend that Standing Orders should allow the Parliament to be able to vote at any time during a business session, to allow for emergency business.

Sittings of the Parliament on Non-Appointed Days and Weekends

21.   Standing Orders should prescribe that all meetings of the Parliament outwith normal prescribed working hours should be called at the discretion of the Presiding Officer.

Provision to Allow Late Sittings of Parliament

22.   Whilst we adhere to the principle of a family-friendly Parliament, observing normal business hours, we recognise the need to provide for exceptional circumstances. We propose that the Standing Orders should allow the Parliament to vote on a motion to continue sitting until current business is completed. Such a motion could be moved by a Minister, the Convener of a Committee or an individual MSP if they had moved the business under consideration. The motion should be both debatable and amendable although amendments should be restricted to suggesting more or less time than specified, and a simple majority of those present and voting should be required for the Parliament's approval. In addition, a time limit for debating such a motion should be prescribed by Standing Orders and time limits for individual speeches during a late sitting should be prescribed.

Provision to Allow Early Sittings of the Parliament

23.   As proposed in paragraph 21, Standing Orders should provide for early sittings of the Parliament to be called at the Presiding Officer's discretion. We considered whether Standing Orders should also prescribe the circumstances in which an early sitting may be called, how much notice should be required to be given to Members to call an early sitting of the Parliament, and how this information will be notified to the Members or whether this should be left to develop through convention. As it is envisaged that this power might be used only in circumstances of exceptional urgency, we concluded that it might be best not to be too prescriptive in Standing Orders.

Suspension of Sittings

24.   There is a fundamental difference between adjourning the Parliament and suspending a sitting. The first is effected by the Parliament itself, with or without debate, according to the Standing Orders. The latter is usually a prerogative of the Chair (Presiding Officer) which may be used in certain (usually unspecified) circumstances.

25.   We propose that, in the main, this matter is left to develop by convention but that a general provision is included in the draft Standing Orders which empowers the Presiding Officer to suspend or close the sitting if he or she considers this is desirable in view of the course of the business or in order to maintain order in the Chamber. Such general provision is currently included in the Standing Orders of some of the Scandinavian countries.

Quorum of the Parliament

26.   Generally no quorum should be required for the Plenary sessions. However, a quorum should be required for votes on matters of particular importance such as the election of the First Minister and Presiding Officer and for the final stage of legislation when a Bill is passed or rejected. Our proposals for quorums are contained in the relevant sections of the report.

Quorum of Parliamentary Committees

27.   Standing Orders should prescribe a quorum which must be reached by Committees both for consideration of business **and** for voting. Given that we are recommending that the number of Members on each Committee may vary between 5 and 15, it is proposed that a quorum of 3 Members is required. Committees which were not quorate would not be able to meet.

Rules of Debate

Scotland Act

28.   Schedule 3 paragraph (1) of the Scotland Act requires the Parliament in its Standing Orders to make provision for preserving order in the proceedings of the Parliament. Provision must be made for (a) preventing conduct which could constitute a criminal offence or contempt of court and (b) a *subjudice* rule. These provisions may also provide for the exclusion of a Member.

Behaviour

29.   It is proposed that the rules governing the behaviour of Members when in Plenary and in Committee should be left to develop through convention. However, we propose that Standing Orders should set out the following 2 general principles which might guide the Parliament:

-   Members should, at all times, conduct themselves in a courteous and respectful manner; and

-   Members should at all times respect the authority of the Chair.

30. The application of such principles is a matter best left to the discretion of the Presiding Officer or the Convener of the relevant Committee, and Standing Orders should remain flexible enough to allow this. The rules governing Members who disrupt proceedings are dealt with in the paragraphs below.

Powers to be Conferred on the Presiding Officer for Preservation of Order

31. As a minimum the Scottish Parliament's Standing Orders should confer the following powers on the Presiding Officer :

- the power to determine the order of speakers whenever necessary;

- the power to set a time limit for speeches in certain types of debate (see below);

- the power to order a Member to discontinue his or her speech if it is repetitive, irrelevant or exceeds set time limits;

- the power to ask a Member to withdraw or to exclude a Member whose conduct is grossly disorderly or could constitute a criminal offence or contempt of court. and

- the power to suspend the Parliament in the case of grave disorder.

32. The approval of the Parliament should be required before the Presiding Officer could exclude a Member from proceedings for more than a day's sitting.

33. Standing Orders should also aim to:

33.1 limit the use of "points of order" to avoid the abuse of this facility; and

33.2 limit the number of times an MSP can speak on an item of business (subject to specific exemptions below).

Determining the Order of Speakers

34. The method used to determine the order of speakers differs throughout Parliaments across Europe. In the Norwegian Parliament speakers will be called in the same order as they catch the President's eye. However, party groups may submit to the President, via the Parliament's secretariat, the names of members who wish to take part in the debate. The President may on the basis of this list then establish the order of the speakers. It is normal for one speaker from each party group to head the list of speakers. In other Scandinavian Parliaments, members add their name to a list in advance, and are simply called in that order.

35. We believe that, ultimately, the order of speakers in the Parliament is a matter best left to the discretion of the Presiding Officer, who should be guided by the principle that all debates should reflect the basic balance of the political parties as well as the rules relating to precedence of speakers during debates (see below). We note, however, that the Presiding Officer might find it helpful, perhaps when determining the need for time limits on speeches and/or particular debates, to have an indication of the number of Members wishing to speak on a specific issue. Therefore, a model along the lines of the Norwegian example above, where Members could register their interest to speak prior to the debate,

might be appropriate. We recommend that generally each main party should have the opportunity to speak in turn at the beginning of a debate.

Interventions During Speeches

36. Interventions during speeches should be allowed only with the agreement of the current speaker. Use of the intervention procedure should be managed by the Presiding Officer under the basic principle that Members should at all times conduct themselves in a courteous and respectful manner. On this basis, no separate Standing Order on interventions would be required.

Use of Quotations During Speeches

37. The use of quotations during speeches in the Scottish Parliament should be left unregulated, as the powers proposed for the Presiding Officer under paragraph 31, ie, to impose time limits on speeches and to order a Member to discontinue his/her speech if it is repetitive or irrelevant, would prove sufficient to curb unnecessary and extensive use of quotations.

Sub judice

38. The Scotland Act requires (schedule 3, paragraph 1(b)) the Standing Orders to include provision for a *sub judice* rule. Such provision may provide for excluding a Member of the Parliament from proceedings.

39. Section 41 provides that for the purposes of the law of defamation, (a), any statement made in proceedings of the Parliament, and (b), the publication under the authority of the Parliament of any statement, shall be absolutely privileged. This is intended to ensure that Members are free to debate matters of public interest (and that such debates can be properly reported) without fear of an action for defamation being raised.

40. Section 42 disapplies the rule of strict liability for contempt of court in relation to publications made in, or in reports of, proceedings of the Scottish Parliament in relation to a Bill or subordinate legislation.

41. The proceedings of the Scottish Parliament, unlike those of Westminster, will be subject to the law of contempt of court. Paragraph 1 of Schedule 3 requires Standing Orders to include provision for preventing conduct which would constitute a criminal offence or contempt of court. Section 42 is intended to ensure that the Scottish Parliament is not prevented from legislating on any matter simply because anything said or done in the proceedings for the purposes of considering a Bill or subordinate legislation might be treated as contempt of court under the "strict liability" rule.

42. It is proposed that a workable *sub judice* rule, provided for in Standing Orders, should:

- be defined in general terms;
- make clear how and by whom it is to be applied;
- impose an explicit duty on members seeking to raise any matter that might infringe that rule to give reasonable notice to the relevant authority and to abide by their ruling; and
- provide that the Presiding Officer should be the "relevant authority".

Form of Address

43. We considered the mode of address which should be adopted in the Scottish Parliament. We looked at 2 main options: reference to other Members in the third party, eg by reference to their constituencies; or reference by name.

44. We noted, however, that the election of regional MSPs under the additional member system proposed for the Scottish Parliament would require some form of address other than by reference to constituency to be identified; reliance on constituency alone would be insufficient and potentially confusing.

45. In the circumstances, we propose that Members of the Scottish Parliament should be addressed simply by name. This convention has been adopted both by the European Parliament and also by the Danish Parliament among others. We recommend that Standing Orders should include only a general provision requiring Members to be addressed respectfully, by name and in the form preferred by the Member eg Mr/Ms/Miss/Mrs Smith/Joan Smith/Joe Smith. This would have the advantage that members of the public and others viewing the proceedings should find it easier to follow the debate.

Time limits on speeches

46. We recommend that no general time limit on speeches should be prescribed by Standing Orders and that the need for a time limit on speeches during certain debates should be left to the discretion of the Presiding Officer, although we suggest that this should be standard practice. The powers proposed for the Presiding Officer under paragraph 31 would allow for this. Enabling Members to register to speak prior to a debate as suggested in paragraphs 34-35 would enable the Presiding Officer to determine when a time limit would need to be imposed. When setting such time limits the Presiding Officer may need to allow additional time for the proponent of a motion or proposal to make his/her case. Some differential allocation of time may also be needed for Members of the Scottish Executive presenting or explaining the Executive's policy.

Precedence in Speeches

47. Standing Orders should include provision to give certain Members, for example Members of the Executive, Committee Conveners (and, if appointed, Committee Reporters), precedence to speak in relevant debates. However, all Members, regardless of their status within their party, should be given the opportunity to participate, subject to the proposals made above. This would be a further reason for the Presiding Officer routinely to set limits on speeches to ensure an adequate balance of time is available to ordinary Members.

Personal Statements

48. We recommend that Standing Orders should include provision to allow Members to make personal statements in the debating Chamber. It is proposed that Members wishing to make such a statement should be required to give notice to the Presiding Officer to allow adequate Parliamentary time to be set aside for the statement.

Should MSPs Speak from their Seat or from a Lectern?

49. We propose that Standing Orders should include provision to require Members to

stand at their seats when addressing the Parliament. Clearly such a provision would not apply to those Members who were disabled. This would enable not only the other Members but also the public to clearly identify the Member speaking.

Access for Officials and other Parliamentary Staff

50.   We propose that Standing Orders should include provision to ensure that Government officials, Parliamentary staff and MSPs' staff, ie all those with legitimate reason, should be given access to designated seats in the debating Chamber. Such access would be dependent on officials and staff possessing a designated security pass, and would also depend on their conducting themselves with discretion while in the Chamber. When in the Chamber they should be allowed to bring necessary messages/papers to Members provided that this is done with discretion.

51.   While in the Chamber, non-Members should **not** be able to sit in those seats allocated to MSPs.

52.   Should a non-Member prove to be disruptive while in the Chamber the Presiding Officer should be allowed to order their exclusion.

Language

53.   We considered the use of Gaelic, Scots and other non-English languages in the Scottish Parliament, and recognised the strong historical and cultural arguments for facilitating the use of Gaelic and Scots in the Parliament.

54.   We agreed that any rules governing the use of language in the Parliament should aim to facilitate MSPs' understanding of, and participation in, the proceedings of the Parliament; and therefore agreed the following recommendations.

55.   We recommend that the normal working language of the Parliament should be English.

56.   We considered the special position of the Scots language, noting that most MSPs can be expected to understand spoken and written Scots, and that many of us switch between Scots and standard English speech depending on the occasion. We expect that this will be the case within the Parliament.

57.   We noted that Ministers have already agreed that there will be provision in the new Parliament building at Holyrood for interpretation and translation facilities; and that these may be used to facilitate the work of MSPs wishing to use Gaelic, as well as on those occasions when a visiting dignitary wishes to address the Parliament in his or her native tongue.

58.   We suggest that Members wishing to make a speech to the Parliament in Gaelic, should give prior notice of their intentions to the Presiding Officer, so that arrangements can be made for interpreting facilities. The provision of these facilities should be at the ultimate discretion of the Presiding Officer, but should be withheld only in extraordinary circumstances. If the Member wishes to use only a phrase or a sentence of the language, he or she should repeat the translation him/herself, to facilitate the understanding of Members.

59.   We propose that no initial provision should be made for interpretation from English into Gaelic or other non-English languages; but that the Parliament itself should decide, once it is established, whether it wishes to make greater provision for interpretation and translation.

60.   We recommend that there should be signage in the Parliament building in both Gaelic and English.

61.   We suggest that no interpretation or translation facilities will be necessary for MSPs wishing to use the Scots language; but that the Presiding Officer should be able to ask for clarification of a particular phrase if he/she feels it necessary.

62.   We recommend that the Official Report of the proceedings of the Parliament should normally be published only in English, and that speeches made in the Parliament in languages other than English and Gaelic should appear in the Official Report only in their English translations. If Parliament so desired, the Parliament could publish the speech in the original language separately.

63.   We recommend that speeches made in the Parliament in Gaelic should be published in the Official Report in the original Gaelic, with an English translation. To assist the Official Report staff, a Member making a speech in Gaelic should submit a copy of the speech in Gaelic and in translation to the Official Report.

64.   We recommend that the Parliament's public information centre should produce regular information bulletins in Gaelic specifically targeted at the Gaelic speaking population; and that they should also produce such bulletins from time-to-time in other non-English languages spoken in Scotland.

Parliamentary Papers

Parliamentary Privilege

64.   Standing Orders should provide for a non-debatable Motion where the Executive seeks the authority of the Parliament to publish papers which would then, through the provisions of section 41 of the Scotland Act, be absolutely privileged for the purposes of the law of defamation. In all other cases it is considered sufficient that all papers not covered by a separate Standing Order (eg Committee reports) presented to Parliament are recorded as having been presented without there being a need to prescribe in Standing Orders how that presentation should take place. Administrative arrangements can be put in place to ensure that the procedures for presenting papers is well known.

The Official Report of Proceedings of the Parliament

65.   Schedule 3 to the Scotland Act requires Standing Orders to include provision for reporting the proceedings of the Parliament.

66.   An official report is the officially-sanctioned record of what is said in the Parliament, both in Plenary session and, in some circumstances, in Committees. We considered whether a transcribed Official Report was required at all. We understand that there are plans to record and televise proceedings in the chamber and Committees, although until the Parliament moves to Holyrood, it is likely that only one Committee room will be equipped

for television. As technology develops, those records might in due course themselves become the Official Report of the Parliament, without the need for transcription, but this is unlikely to be feasible in the near future.

67.   We propose that a transcribed written record of proceedings should be available both on the Internet and in print. Transcribed text can more easily be used for a range of other purposes (eg, constituent-friendly summaries) and it enables indexing and retrieval of specific references. The courts can in certain circumstances refer to Hansard (the Official Report at Westminster) in construing legislation and the Official Report of the Scottish Parliament may be used in a similar way.

The Style of the Official Report

68.   There are various options for the style of the Official Report: purely verbatim, with no editing; "substantially verbatim", such as the Hansard used at Westminster, where text is edited to filter out unnecessary wording and to make the report generally more readable; and summary reports. We recommend that the Parliament should produce some sort of summary report, perhaps edited highlights of each week's proceedings, but we do not think that could itself form the Official Report and it would in any case be necessary first to have produced a more substantial report from which the edited highlights would be taken. We recommend that a substantially verbatim Official Report of Plenary sessions should be produced.

69.   Most who will require working copies are likely to use electronic means, but we consider that a version should also be available in print for those who do not have access to technology. We suggest that a daily printed version will not be necessary, particularly if, as we propose, the Parliament were to meet in Plenary session on only 2 days each week. In those circumstances, a weekly version would suffice and we recommend that the Parliament should consider options for printing that produce an acceptable permanent record without incurring unjustified costs. This should be in addition to the edited highlights suggested above, since verbatim reports would not be particularly constituent-friendly.

Committee Reports

70.   For some of their time, Committees will be sitting relatively informally, discussing work plans, draft reports, etc. No Official Report will be required for those sittings; the Clerk should simply produce a note of points made and decisions taken.   On other occasions, Committees will be hearing evidence from members and staff of the Executive and other witnesses. In these cases we believe that a verbatim report of oral evidence will be required, but that it will not have to be available immediately, particularly since witnesses will have to be given the opportunity to agree it.

71.   Committees will also be considering legislation. One possibility is that procedures will follow the Westminster model, whereby Committees with the relevant Minister scrutinise Bills line by line and discussion is reported verbatim. An alternative more European model would be for a Committee to scrutinise a Bill and to make its considered report to Parliament together with the amended Bill. Such reports would be drafted by the Committee clerks, with no need for verbatim reporting of proceedings in Committee. We understand, however, that the legal profession finds verbatim reports of Committee consideration helpful in indicating what a particular provision is intended to mean. We

assume, therefore, that Official Reports may be required. If such reports did not have to be available the next day, there could be cost savings, since they could be transcribed on non-sitting days. We therefore propose that any Committee reports required should not have to be available the next day, but that they should be available in electronic form in good time for the next meeting of that Committee. They would be printed at a subsequent date.

Summary of recommendations for Standing Orders

The Standing Orders should provide that:

- the Business Committee should put a regular programme of business to the Parliament for the Parliament to approve. This might be done on a weekly basis looking at the forthcoming two weeks. The Business motion should be debatable but the debate on it should be time limited. Members should be able to table amendments to the Business Programme, provided a minimum of 10 MSPs subscribe to the amendment.

- a minimum amount of time of 12 days per year should be allocated for non-Executive business.

- time should be set aside at the end of each Plenary day for Private Members' business.

- the Business Committee should allocate time for Private Members' Bills.

- a minimum amount of Parliamentary time should be set aside for Committee business.

- Members should have a right to table motions, which should be published.

- Committees should not sit when the Plenary is in session.

- the Parliament should normally meet between the hours of 9.30am and 5.30pm on Tuesday to Thursday; 2.30pm to 5.30pm on Monday; and 9.30am to 12.30pm on Friday;

- the Parliament should be in Recess for a specified number of weeks per year which would enable it to break for party conferences and the Scottish school holidays.

- Committees should be able to meet at other times when the Plenary itself is not in session.

- voting should take place each day at 5.00pm, except for votes on legislation and election of officers, and for emergency business.

- all meetings of the Parliament outwith normal prescribed working hours should be called at the discretion of the Presiding Officer.

- the Parliament should be able to vote on a motion to continue sitting until current business is completed. Such a motion could be moved by a Minister, the Convener of a Committee or an individual MSP if they had moved the business under consideration. The motion would be both debatable and amendable although amendments would be restricted to suggesting more or less time than specified, and a simple majority of those present and voting would be required for the Parliament's approval. In addition, a time limit for debating such a motion should be prescribed by Standing Orders and time limits for individual speeches during a late sitting should be prescribed.

- the Presiding Officer should be able to suspend or close any sitting of the Parliament if he or she considers this is desirable in view of the course of business or in order to maintain order in the Chamber.

- a quorum of 3 members should be required for a Committee to meet.

- Members should, at all times, conduct themselves in a courteous and respectful manner.

- Members should at all times respect the authority of the Chair.

- the Presiding Officer should be given the following powers:

  - the power to determine the order of speakers whenever necessary;

  - the power to set a time limit for speeches in certain types of debate;

  - the power to order a Member to discontinue his or her speech if it is repetitive, irrelevant or exceeds set time limits;

  - the power to ask a Member to withdraw or to exclude a Member whose conduct is grossly disorderly or could constitute a criminal offence or contempt of court; and

  - the power to suspend the Parliament in the case of grave disorder.

- the approval of the Parliament should be necessary before the Presiding Officer could exclude a member for more than a day's sitting.

- there should be a role on *sub judice* which should:

  - be defined in general terms;

  - make clear how and by whom it is to be applied;

  - impose an explicit duty on members seeking to raise any matter that might infringe that rule to give reasonable notice to the relevant authority and to abide by their ruling; and

  - provide that the Presiding Officer should be the "relevant authority".

- Members should be addressed respectfully and in the form preferred by them.

- there should be provision to give certain Members, for example Members of the Executive, Committee Conveners (and, if appointed, Committee Reporters), precedence to speak in relevant debates.

- Members should be able to make personal statements in the chamber, having given prior notice to the Presiding Officer.

- Members should normally stand at their seats when addressing the Parliament.

- Government officials, Parliamentary staff and MSPs' staff, ie all those with legitimate reason, should be given access to designated seats in the debating Chamber. Such access would be dependent on officials and staff possessing a designated security pass, and would also depend on their conducting themselves with discretion while in the Chamber. When in the Chamber they should be allowed to bring necessary messages/papers to Members provided that this is done with discretion.

- while in the Chamber, non-Members should **not** be able to sit in those seats allocated to MSPs.

- should a non-Member prove to be disruptive while in the Chamber it is proposed that the Presiding Officer should be allowed to order their exclusion.

- the proceedings of the Parliament should be published in an Official Report.

- Standing Orders should also aim to:

  - limit the use of "points of order" to avoid the abuse of this facility; and

  - limit the number of times an MSP may speak on an item of business.

SECTION 3.4:

ACCOUNTABILITY

Introduction

1. One of our key principles relates to accountability and we believe that much of the work of the Parliament will focus on scrutinising the Scottish Executive in exercising its functions. This section considers the various ways in which the Parliament and individual MSPs might hold the Scottish Executive to account. The question of accountability of members is considered in section 3.2 (on members).

Holding the Executive to Account : the Full Parliament

Annual Report and Budget

2. The Scottish Executive will be expected to announce its forward legislative programme for the Parliamentary session soon after each general election. This announcement, which would be detailed in respect of the forthcoming year and more aspirational in respect of the following years, should be subject to a debate in the Plenary. In addition we recommend that the Executive should be able to come forward during a session with a revised programme should it need to respond to a change in circumstances. Standing Orders should also require the Executive to inform the Parliament annually of its planned timetable for legislation.

3. It is important that the statements made by the Executive should go wider than simply referring to the Executive's legislative proposals. In an annual statement to the Parliament, the Executive should be required to outline its main aims, objectives and policy priorities, and the various means, administrative, Executive, legislative, by which it intends to achieve them. If possible, this might look beyond one year, but could be updated annually. The statement might take the form of an annual report, reporting on progress made in the previous year, changes in approaches etc. Thus it would include an element of performance review, and appropriate performance indicators would need to be set.

4. It is proposed that any such statement from the Executive should be the subject of a debate in Plenary session on a motion to approve the programme. This motion would be open to amendment. The length of such a debate should be a matter for the Parliament to decide.

5. A similar annual statement should be made in respect of the Executive's financial proposals, also subject to debate in Plenary, although this would be a separate event. Again this would be debated on a motion to approve the statement, which would be open to amendment.

General Debates

6. It is assumed that the Parliament will wish to hold debates from time to time on matters of public policy, during which the Executive will be expected to set out and defend its

policy position. Some such debates may be initiated by the Executive, others by non-Executive parties, by Committees or by a specified minimum number of Members. The Business Committee would be involved in programming such debates but we recommend that the Standing Orders should provide for some guarantee for a minimum amount of time to non-Executive parties and Committees (see section 3.3).

Ministerial Statements

7. Standing Orders should provide for the First Minister and the Scottish Ministers to make special Ministerial Statements to the Parliament on matters of public interest. Such statements would be made early in the day's business and should be followed by a short debate. The debate might be either subject to a time limit or could be added to the end of the day's business (to avoid programmed business being disrupted too much). We considered whether Ministers should be forced to make a statement on a particular issue of public interest, perhaps following a request from a minimum number of MSPs, but concluded that the "Emergency" Question (see below) would achieve the same effect.

Votes of No Confidence

8. Any Member should be able to present a motion for a vote of no confidence either in the entire Executive or in a named Minister, which must be debated and voted upon provided they have the support of a specified minimum number of at least 26 MSPs. Any such motion would be both debatable and amendable. It is stipulated in the Scotland Act that the First Minister must tender his/her resignation and the Scottish Ministers and Junior Scottish Ministers must resign if the Executive no longer enjoys the confidence of the Parliament. However, should the Parliament pass a motion of no confidence in a named Minister, this would not automatically lead to the resignation of the Minister concerned.

Holding the Executive to Account : Committees

9. Under our recommendations, Committees should be able to scrutinise the activities of the Executive in a number of ways: for example, they should have the power to conduct enquiries and to take oral and written evidence from Ministers, Civil Servants and others. In addition to these methods, the paragraphs below propose a number of other mechanisms which Committees may adopt in order to scrutinise the Executive.

Role of Committees in the Policy Development and Pre-Legislative Processes

10. The policy development, pre-legislative process is described fully in section 3.5. Paragraph 2 above proposes that the Executive should be required to make an annual report to the Parliament which should be the subject of a debate in Plenary. In addition to this, we propose that individual Ministers should be invited to address the relevant subject Committees on the detail of the relevant parts of the Executive's proposals, perhaps outlining in more detail their aims and objectives; their plans for taking things forward; the main thrust of any proposed legislation; and the consultation which the Executive plans to undertake. This would provide Committees with a valuable opportunity to influence the development of policy at the very earliest stages and would also inform the Executive again at an early stage of any reservations or concerns the Committee was likely to have on a particular issue.

11. The role of Committees in terms of scrutinising the Executive's financial proposals

and in considering EU policy, and draft European Union legislation, is considered in the attached Appendix and in paragraphs 28-32 below.

"Taking Stock" Meetings

12. The Standing Orders of the Catalonian Parliament make provision for Government Ministers to attend "Taking Stock" Meetings in Committees. These meetings may take place either at the request of the Minister or at the request of the Committee. Such meetings provide an opportunity for Government Ministers to update Committees on the general progress and performance of their Ministry and are in the main for information only. We believe that such stock-taking meetings might be useful, and would not require specific provision in Standing Orders. If either a Committee or a Minister felt that such a meeting would be useful, it is unlikely that the other would disagree, subject to agreement as to timing. This should be left to the Parliament to develop.

Holding the Executive to Account : Individual MSPs

13. Oral and written Parliamentary Questions (PQs) will provide an important means for individual Members to obtain information from the Executive and to hold the Executive to account. The time provided in Plenary for Parliamentary Questions should not be used for political points scoring. PQs should be used genuinely to elicit information. The paragraphs below consider the detail of how Parliamentary Questions might be submitted, selected and answered.

Arrangements for Submitting Written PQs

14. The detail of the arrangements for submitting written Parliamentary Questions differs slightly from country to country across Europe. However, almost all Standing Orders on this issue contain the following :

> 14.1 a general provision stating that questions must be as brief as possible and must not contain offensive language;
>
> 14.2 a designated person/office to whom/which questions must be officially submitted;
>
> 14.3 a time limit by which written answers must be provided; and
>
> 14.4 a provision requiring all questions and answers to be recorded in a Parliamentary publication.

15. We recommend that the Scottish Parliament's Standing Orders on this matter contain, as a minimum, all four of these elements.

16. We considered whether questions should be accepted only if they relate to matters for which the Executive is responsible, or whether any questions should be allowable, with the form of answer remaining at the discretion of the Executive. On the one hand, limiting questions to those concerning matters for which the Scottish Executive is responsible would reduce the volume of questions being asked, and avoid wasting the Parliament's and Executive's time answering questions which were not within the Executive's responsibility. On the other hand, it would be open to Members to phrase questions in such a way as to make them acceptable. For example, a question such as "What is the Scottish Executive's

policy in respect of the situation in Afghanistan?", would not be accepted or relevant. However, "When was the last time the First Minister discussed the situation in Afghanistan with a Member of the UK Government?" might be. If Ministers consistently replied to such questions with "this is a matter for the UK Government... ", it is hoped that MSPs would learn through experience what matters were worth pursuing by the PQ mechanism and which should be pursued by other means. However, some guidance to Clerks on the acceptability of questions would be essential to assist the smooth processing of business.

17. The Scottish Parliament will almost certainly have some form of Parliamentary Office which will fulfil the functions carried out by a number of offices at Westminster, including the Table Office. It is proposed therefore that all Parliamentary Questions are submitted to this office. Once questions have been submitted it would be for the Clerks to advise on whether questions were in the correct format etc. and to ensure that both questions and answers were printed in the appropriate Parliamentary publication.

18. We suggest that PQs should be addressed in the first instance to the Scottish Ministers and it would be for the First Minister to allocate questions to particular Ministers for reply. Where information was readily available in the public domain, members should be able to address questions seeking such information to the Parliament's Information Centre.

19. We considered whether Standing Orders should go beyond that suggested above and include more detailed provision, for example to disallow questions to which answers have been given in the last 3-6 months (in Westminster the period is 12 months), to allow questions not answered within a set time limit to then be raised orally and to allow Ministers to choose to answer orally a question which would ordinarily require to be answered in writing. We can see arguments in favour of prescribing such rules in the initial Standing Orders. Alternatively, such matters could be left to develop through convention.

Arrangements for Submitting Oral PQs

20. Notice of Parliamentary Questions for oral answer should be submitted to the relevant office in the same way as written questions but that the questioner must indicate that the question is for oral rather than written answer. It is envisaged that appropriate templates would be provided. Five working days notice would be required to be given prior to an oral question being raised in the Chamber. Provision should be made for Members to submit questions electronically. All questions should be typewritten.

Allocation of Days and Time for Oral PQs

21. The allocation of days and time for oral PQs will, to a large extent, depend on the sitting pattern which the Parliament chooses to adopt. However, based on the sitting pattern proposed in section 3.3, it is suggested that a regular weekly Question Time could be scheduled as the first item of business following lunch on a Thursday afternoon, lasting perhaps for 20 minutes to half an hour. This would ensure that a large number of Members were present for the start of the afternoon Plenary session.

22. There are also a number of detailed issues to take into account. We propose that the order of the questions to be asked on a particular day should be determined by random selection by computer. Questions which are not reached during a particular session should be given a written answer. We considered what provision should be made in relation to

supplementary questions ie should a maximum number of supplementary questions be permitted, should the number of supplementaries and the number of times a Member can speak be limited. We concluded that this should be left to the discretion of the Presiding Officer, bearing in mind the overall time limit for questions.

23.   We propose that each Oral Question Time should cover all members of the Scottish Executive rather than having a rota of questions on specific Ministerial portfolios. This would ensure that questions on topical issues could be pursued.

Arrangements for "Emergency" Oral PQs

24.   In the House of Commons any Member may submit an "Emergency" oral PQ or Private Notice Question (PNQ). These questions usually relate to matters of public importance and must be submitted before 12 noon. The Speaker then decides whether the question should be debated on the floor of the House that afternoon. If so, Members are notified that a debate will take place.

25.   We considered the level of provision which should be included in the Scottish Parliament's Standing Orders in relation to this issue. In particular we considered whether all Members, or a minimum number of Members, should be able to submit such a question, whether it should be for the Business Committee or the Presiding Officer to take a decision on which questions will be allowed and whether a time limit should be imposed on the discussion of the question. We concluded that it should be for the Presiding Officer to decide whether such questions should be allowed as s/he would be expected to act with impartiality.

Adjournment Type Debates

26.   We propose in section 3.3 that time should be set aside following voting on Wednesday and Thursday afternoons for non-Executive business similar to Westminster's Adjournment debates. This would provide individual Members with an additional opportunity to question the Executive on mainly constituency related business.

Financial Issues

27.   The Scotland Act requires the Scottish Parliament to make rules covering the preparation of its accounts, procedures for independent audit and arrangements for the submission of reports to the Parliament. In addition the Parliament needs procedures for approving expenditure for using the tax varying power, for overseeing the work of the auditors and for scrutinising the outputs obtained from the expenditure required to be considered. We endorse the recommendations of the Financial Issues Advisory Group, a summary of which is set out in Annex I.

European Issues

Scrutiny of EU Legislative Proposals

28.   The Scottish Parliament will be able to scrutinise all EU documentation deposited at Westminster, to ensure that Scotland's interests are properly taken into account in the development of the UK line. The volume of documents lodged is considerable (Westminster typically deals with around 800 separate documents per annum). It is

therefore unlikely that the Scottish Parliament will be able to consider all of them in equal detail, notwithstanding the time constraints mentioned above.

29.   It is thus essential that scrutiny procedures are able effectively to sift documents, to identify which are of most interest to Scotland and to identify those where the Parliament's influence can best be brought to bear (recognising that in practice the scrutiny process gives limited influence in a process which also involves Council of Ministers meetings, officials' working groups and the European Parliament).

30.   We recommend:

30.1   the Parliament should establish a separate European Committee whose membership should be drawn from members of other relevant Committees (eg covering agriculture, fisheries, the environment, transport) (see section 3.2);

30.2   Membership of the Committee will necessarily be limited. However, any Member of the Parliament should be able to speak at Committee meetings, though they would not count towards the quorum, make formal proposals or vote;

30.3   the Committee should have 2 main roles: firstly to act as a sifting mechanism on EU documents and other material; and secondly to debate issues which either do not fall to any subject Committee, or which fall to several and where it would be helpful to hold a single debate. Furthermore, the Committee should be prepared to take a proactive role in the development of key areas of EU policy;

30.4.   in assessing subjects for debate, the Committee should take into account, *inter alia*: the importance to Scotland of the issue involved, the relative importance of Scottish activity to the UK as a whole or to the EU; the time available for debate before the relevant Council of Ministers takes place, the time available for debate before the UK view is formulated; and more generally the political importance or sensitivity of the subject;

30.5   initial sifting recommendations should be made by the Committee Convener and reporters.   The final decision on what action if any to take on these items (eg referral to the subject Committee, debate in Plenary, or further enquiry within the European Committee) should be made by the Committee as a whole;

30.6   each Committee member should be provided with access to the full list of documents deposited and this should also be made available to all members. Any Committee member should be able to request further information on an item, or to propose that it be debated at the Committee to assess whether further action need be taken on it;

30.7   the Committee should call for evidence from officials and Ministers of the Executive, from interest groups in Scotland and from other parties, including inviting evidence from the European Commission. Such evidence could take the form of written submissions or personal evidence, as appropriate.

30.8   the Committee should be able to sit in wider forum, or take advice from specialist advisory groups, where it was helpful for evidence from a variety of invitees to be considered simultaneously; and

30.9   the Committee should develop close links with its counter-parts in Westminster, Cardiff and Belfast.

Implementation of EU Legislation

31.   In relation to the implementation of EU legislation, where responsibility falls to the Scottish Executive, the Parliament and its Committees will have an essential role in assessing modes of implementation and their success once they are in place. However, it is likely that much of the assessment of implementation arrangements will fall to individual subject Committees, rather than primarily to the European Committee. The latter may, however, wish to retain a broad overview of how successfully the Executive was implementing EU requirements.

Pre- and Post-Council Briefings

32.   We recommend that the Business Committee should have the flexibility to decide in conjunction with the European Committee, whether a debate prior to a Council meeting was necessary or relevant. We believe that some form of post-Council feedback, to the Plenary or relevant Committee, should be the norm.

Links with Europe

33.   We recommend that the Parliament should consider establishing links with other devolved Parliaments in Europe and with the European Parliament, to consider areas of common interest. In particular the Parliament should consider establishing links between MSPs and Scottish Members of the European Parliament, together with Scottish representatives in other relevant European bodies, to facilitate the exchange of information and views on European Union issues affecting Scotland.

Summary of Recommendations of Standing Orders

Standing Orders should provide that:

- an annual policy statement from the Executive should be the subject of a debate in Plenary session on a motion to approve the programme, which motion would be open to amendment. The length of such a debate should be a matter for the Parliament to decide.

- there should be a similar annual statement and debate in respect of the Executive's financial proposals.

- the First Minister and the Scottish Ministers should be able to make special Ministerial Statements to the Parliament on matters of public interest.

- in respect of Parliamentary Questions the Standing Orders provisions should include:

  - a general provision stating that questions must be as brief as possible and must not contain offensive language;

  - a designated person/office to whom/which questions must be officially submitted;

  - a time limit by which written answers must be provided; and

  - a provision requiring all questions and answers to be recorded in a Parliamentary publication.

- PQs should be addressed in the first instance to the Scottish Ministers.

- notice of Parliamentary Questions for oral answer should be submitted to the relevant office as should written questions but that the questioner must indicate that the question is for oral rather than written answer. Five working days notice should be required.

- there should be a regular weekly Question Time following lunch on a Thursday afternoon.

- the order of the questions to be asked on a particular day should be determined by random selection by computer. Questions which are not reached during a particular session should be given a written answer.

- each Oral Question Time should cover all members of the Scottish Executive rather than having a rota of questions on specific Ministerial portfolios.

- there should be provision for emergency PQs.

Our detailed recommendations on financial issues are set out in the attached Annex I.

SECTION 3.5:

THE LEGISLATIVE PROCESS

Introduction

1. In considering the detailed process through which legislation should be made in the Scottish Parliament, we have been influenced in particular by our key principles of power-sharing and of access and participation. It is important that those most affected by legislation should have the opportunity to influence the development of the policy leading up to the legislation. We therefore propose an important role for Committees in the scrutiny process. We have also sought to ensure that the Executive is fully accountable to the Parliament on the legislation, both primary and secondary, which it introduces. Finally, we have sought to ensure that there are adequate arrangements in place to enable Committees to initiate legislation, and for individual Members to put forward proposals.

Primary Legislation

2. One of the things that will distinguish the Scottish Parliament from other devolved assemblies is the fact that it will be able to enact primary legislation on a wide range of issues affecting Scotland. While we do not envisage that the Parliament will have to pass significant numbers of Acts of the Scottish Parliament each year, we expect that certainly in the first few years it might choose to consider 10-12 Bills each year, together with a heavy load of secondary legislation. This section sets out our proposals for the policy development and pre-legislative process; the 3 stages of a Bill; legislation originating in the Executive, Committee and the individual Member; secondary legislation and private legislation.

The policy development process

3. The design of a uni-cameral Scottish Parliament has led many to focus on the important role that Committees may play as the "revising Chamber" in scrutinising draft legislation. While our proposals for Committees recognise the need for a strong role for Committees in considering legislation, we believe that there is a need to extend the process to form a recognised policy-development stage. This has been echoed in many of the submissions made to us. A formal, well-structured, well-understood process would not only deliver a scrutiny stage pre-Introduction, but would also allow individuals and groups to influence the policy-making process at a much earlier stage than at present. By making the system more participative, it is intended that better legislation should result.

4. Consultation, in the form of inviting comments on specific legislative proposals for example, would not meet our aspirations for a participative policy development process. We have noted elsewhere that there is a perception among those we consulted (and within our own group) that once detailed legislative proposals have been published, in whatever form, it is extremely difficult for outside organisations to influence changes to those proposals to any great extent. What is desired is an earlier involvement of relevant bodies from the outset - identifying issues which need to be addressed, contributing to the policy-making process and the preparation of legislation.

5. There appears to be little doubt that, while Members and Committees in the Scottish Parliament will have the power to initiate legislation, the majority of legislation will originate from the Executive. This is the case in the various Parliaments we have looked at. Given that there should be some form of participative involvement in the development of legislative proposals, we recommend that Standing Orders should require Executive Bills to complete a consultative process before being presented to Parliament. The role of the Committee would essentially be a monitoring/enforcing role to ensure the requirement is met. The Committee would always remain able to take evidence relating to the legislative proposals if it felt that the Executive's consultation process had been insufficient.

6. Under this model, the relevant Minister would inform the relevant Committee of the Government's legislative intentions in its area, including discussion about which relevant bodies should be involved in the consultation process. The Executive would, in consultation with the appropriate bodies, identify the issues to be addressed and the policy to be introduced. The Committee should be kept informed of progress. When the draft legislation is introduced by the Executive, Standing Orders should require such drafts to be accompanied by a memorandum explaining the need for the legislation, the options considered, the consultative process undertaken, and the degree of consensus reached. Committees would be able to monitor the Executive's performance in this area, and to take additional evidence if necessary. The benefits of this model include:

- involving relevant bodies in the development of policy and the legislative process at an early stage;

- allowing the Executive, as the elected Government, to take forward its policies;

- ensuring proper participative consultation by the Executive through giving Committees a supervisory role;

- freeing up valuable Committee time, allowing Committees to focus on proposals which have already been the subject of participative involvement of interested bodies.

Introduction of a Bill

7. We recommend that the Scottish Parliament should have the ability to require Bills to be presented in a particular form. We favour the model used in some continental Parliaments where a Bill is prefixed by a memorandum (separate from the preamble which forms part of the completed Act) explaining:

- the nature of the problem it is intended to address, and the strategic approach;

- the options considered, and why this particular option was chosen;

- the consultative process undertaken;

- the best estimated costs, benefits and financial implications;

- possibly, such other criteria as the impact on sustainable development, equal opportunities, implications for Islands communities, human rights and business cost compliance.

8. Before or on the introduction of a Bill, the Presiding Officer is required by section 31 of the Scotland Act to decide whether or not, in his or her view, the provisions of the Bill would be within the legislative competence of the Parliament, and to state his or her decision.

9. We propose that a Bill should not be introduced before the draft Bill is first referred to the Presiding Officer for his or her consideration. The interpretation of the legislative competence of the Parliament is legally complex and cases may arise where there is genuine uncertainty as to where the boundary should be drawn. The Presiding Officer may want to consult a legal adviser before reaching his or her decision, but that need not be prescribed in Standing Orders. Standing Orders should provide for the form of the statement of a decision by the Presiding Officer on legislative competence to the Parliament and for it to be published.

Stages of a Bill

10. The Scotland Act (section 36) requires Standing Orders to provide 3 stages in the consideration of a Bill. We recommend that Stage 1, debate and vote on the principles of the Bill, should be conducted in Plenary. A Bill, once introduced, should be referred to the relevant Committee, which should consider and report on the general principles in the Bill, to inform a debate and vote on the principles of the Bill in the Plenary session.

11. The role of the Committee as proposed would be to provide a report to the Parliament as to whether or not the Bill should be approved in principle. It would not at this stage be a detailed consideration on a line by line basis of the Bill's content. At this stage, the Committee would also be able to comment on the Memorandum accompanying the Bill, in particular on the extent of consultation undertaken, and to recommend whether further evidence should be taken to inform the next stage of consideration of the Bill.

12. Following a debate and positive vote in Plenary on the principles of the Bill, the Bill should be referred again to Committee for detailed consideration. Where there are 2 or more interested Committees, one Committee should be identified as the "lead" and other interested Committees should submit their views to the lead Committee within a specified time.

13. A specified period should be required to elapse between the debate and vote in Plenary on the principles of the Bill, and detailed consideration in Committee. During this period all MSPs should have the opportunity to propose amendments to the Bill, which would require to be considered in Committee. If further evidence were to be taken, it should be done during this period.

14. Committee stage should be able to be taken by the Plenary rather than being remitted to an individual subject Committee.

15. The third stage of the Bill should be a debate and final vote on the Bill, as amended in Committee. The Bill returned to the Plenary from the subject Committee should be accompanied by a report explaining the Committee's reasons for the amendments made. Plenary should then consider the Committee report. Further amendments should be allowed at this stage. Standing Orders should specify tight criteria for what sorts of amendments might be moved. The Bill as then amended should in Plenary session be passed or rejected

by the Scottish Parliament. A quorum of Members, equivalent to at least 25% of the total number of seats, would be required to vote, to allow a final decision on a Bill to be taken on a simple majority vote.

16.   Where the Judicial Committee of the Privy Council has decided that a Bill, or any of its provisions, are outwith the legislative competence of the Scottish Parliament, (or where the Secretary of State has made an order prohibiting the Presiding Officer from submitting the Bill for Royal Assent) the Bill or its relevant provisions would have to be amended. It should be open to the Executive to propose to withdraw the Bill at this stage, subject to the Parliament's agreement. If the Executive does not withdraw the Bill, then the Bill should be remitted to the relevant Committee for amendment to address the problem identified by the JCPC, before being approved or rejected by the Parliament.

17.   Standing Orders should allow for the minimum requirements for gaps between stages of Bills, and for proceedings to be expedited in the case of Bills which the Parliament agrees are emergency Bills. For example, it might not be necessary to remit such a Bill to Committee before the debate and vote on the principle of the Bill. Such Bills, needed to deal with emergency situations, might be introduced by a member of the Scottish Executive as an "urgent Bill", put to the vote, and if accepted as an urgent Bill by the Parliament, should be subject to a shortened scrutiny.

Bills Initiated in Committee

18.   The SCC report and the White Paper "Scotland's Parliament" envisaged the possibility of Bills being initiated by Committees of the Parliament. We endorse the proposal that Committees should have the power to initiate legislation (see section 3.2).

19.   We recommend that Committees of the Scottish Parliament should have the capacity to conduct inquiries (which would include the taking of written and oral evidence) on the need for legislation or further legislation in any area within their terms of reference. The Committees should report on such inquiries, with recommendations; such reports might include reference to the matters on which the Scottish Executive is required to provide information when promoting a public Bill (in a manner consistent with a legislative proposal as opposed to a draft Bill). In a Plenary session, the Scottish Parliament would adopt, or reject, the Report. The question of what should happen then needs to be clarified. If the Executive were required to provide a response to such Committee reports, before the Plenary debate, then it should be clear whether the Executive intended to introduce legislation on the lines proposed. If not, then the adoption of the Report by the Parliament should provide authority for the legislation to be drafted, within a given time if that is specified by the resolution of the Parliament. The Committee Convener should be authorised to instruct the preparation of a Bill on behalf of the Committee, within a given time if that is specified by the resolution of the Parliament. If the Executive indicated that it would bring forward the relevant legislation, then the Committee should not proceed to instruct.

20.   Following introduction and a general debate and vote on the Bill in Plenary session, the Bill should follow the same procedure as proposed above for Bills proposed by the Executive with the exception that the detailed scrutiny of the Bill at its Committee stage might be undertaken in Plenary session.

Private Members' Bills

21.   Individual Members should be entitled to submit written proposals for legislation to the Presiding Officer. Such proposals should be brought before the Plenary if either they could secure the support of a minimum number of MSPs (perhaps 10% of the total), or by submitting them to the relevant subject Committee which should then have a discretionary competence to initiate an inquiry on the need for such legislation and to report to the Scottish Parliament. We also recommend that individual members should be able to introduce no more than 2 Bills in any Parliamentary session.

Legislative session

22.   We propose that the Scottish Parliament should adopt a 4-year legislative session. This would allow more time for proper scrutiny and would avoid important Bills being "lost" at the end of the annual cycle.

23.   It is proposed elsewhere in this report that the Executive should announce its forward legislative programme for the full Parliamentary session soon after each election.   (In practical terms, this would most likely be when Parliament resumed following the summer recess after the May election.)   It should, however, be open to the Executive to come forward with a revised programme from time to time throughout the session, to enable it to respond to changing circumstances.   Indeed, the Executive should be required to inform Parliament annually of its planned timetable for bringing forward legislation.

Bills - Queen's Consent

24.   Schedule 3, paragraph 7 of the Scotland Act requires that Standing Orders provide for ensuring that a Bill containing provisions which would, if the Bill were a Bill for an Act of the UK Parliament, require the consent of Her Majesty, the Prince and Steward of Scotland or the Duke of Cornwall, shall not pass unless such consent has been signified to the Parliament.

25.   It is proposed that, in the case of Executive Bills, the onus should be placed on Departments of the Executive to recognise that consent should be sought, and arrange for the First Minister to write requesting the necessary consent from Her Majesty. In the case of Private Members' Bills and Committee Bills we propose that the office of the Parliament which handles legislation should alert the Private Member or the Committee Convener who would ask either the First Minister or the Presiding Officer to obtain Queen's Consent.

26.   Once Her Majesty's consent has been received, the Presiding Officer should be notified and should ensure that a note was put on the Order Paper, stating that Her Majesty's Consent has been signified. To ensure accuracy, the Clerk of the Parliament (or one of his or her assistants) could endorse the record copy of the Bill.

Subordinate Legislation

27.   The Interpretation Act 1978 describes subordinate legislation as "Orders in Council, orders, rules, regulations, schemes, warrants, bylaws and other instruments made or to be made under any Act".   Generally speaking, subordinate legislation allows the Executive (subject to Parliamentary approval) to fill in the details of the implementation of policy already agreed by the Parliament in primary legislation.

Position

28.   Until such time as the Scottish Parliament chooses to make its own legislation to provide for the passage of subordinate legislation through the Parliament, the Statutory Instruments Act 1946, with modifications to suit the circumstances of the Scottish Parliament, will be applied. Initially, Standing Orders will have to reflect the transitional arrangements, although such Standing Orders may need to be adjusted should the Scottish Parliament decide to enact its own legislation.

General

29.   It is common at Westminster for detailed implementing provisions to be prescribed in secondary legislation. Such provision can have a significant impact on those affected by the provisions. Because of the volume of secondary legislation it is often difficult for interested groups and individuals to keep track of proposals, and consultation on secondary legislation is limited. There should be meaningful consultation on secondary legislation before it is laid before the Scottish Parliament. The Parliament should seek to ensure that significant provisions are included in primary rather than secondary legislation.

Committees

30.   We propose that all subordinate legislation from the Executive which is required to be laid in the Parliament, should be sent both to the relevant subject Committee and to a delegated legislation Committee, similar to the current Joint Committee on Statutory Instruments (JCSI) which serves both Houses at Westminster. Such a Committee would have two main functions: it would examine the provisions within Bills conferring powers to make subordinate legislation, and it would examine subordinate legislation brought before the Parliament, not from a policy perspective but to assess whether it was *intra-vires*. The Committee would be able to report its concerns on any technical aspect of subordinate legislation.

31.   All subordinate legislation should be passed to the subject Committee, which would want to consider all subordinate legislation coming before it. However the Committee would neither want, nor be able, to debate all subordinate legislation in detail. It is proposed that the Committee might look at a weekly list of all subordinate legislation submitted and consider which it would like to examine in more detail perhaps in debate. It would be informed by reports from the Committee on subordinate legislation. In the case of affirmative Statutory Instruments (where the approval of the Parliament will be necessary) it is likely that the Committee would want to consider the proposed legislation and report to the Parliament with its recommendations. In the case of Statutory Instruments subject to negative resolution, the Committee would have 40 days to decide whether it wished to oppose the piece of legislation. The Committee could choose to debate the SI in Committee, with a report and a motion going to Plenary as a result of the Committee debate. If the Committee felt that the legislation, or their concerns about it, were of sufficient significance   that they wanted the legislation to be debated in Plenary, the Committee would indicate this to the Business Committee.

32.   It will of course be open to all MSPs to "pray against" negative subordinate legislation. (The term is used in the Statutory Instruments Act 1946, and means simply that Members may indicate their objection to a piece of subordinate legislation. The term "pray against" must be used until the Scottish Parliament decides its own legislation. We

recommend that in any new provisions, more accessible language should be used.) In the first instance MSPs should indicate their concerns to the relevant Committee, which could consider whether it wished to debate the legislation and consider whether it wished to recommend that the Plenary should be asked to vote on the legislation. MSPs would be able to explain their concerns to the Committee. It would also be open to MSPs to make their views known to the Business Committee if they felt that legislation should be debated in Plenary.

33. It is also proposed that, if debate on an affirmative SI has taken place in Committee and a report laid before the Parliament, there is less need for further debate to take place in Plenary, unless such consideration is recommended by the subject Committee or the Business Committee. A vote should normally suffice. A similar procedure should be put in place for negative SIs where the Committee recommends annulment. No action would be required if the Committee had agreed that no opposition should be made.

Private Legislation

34. In Scotland, when local authorities or other bodies (eg Railtrack) wish to obtain Parliamentary powers, they may proceed through the promotion of a draft Provisional Order under the Private Legislation Procedure (Scotland) Act 1936. The detailed procedures which deal with Scottish private legislation are laid down in a set of General Orders (the equivalent of Standing Orders) under the 1936 Act. It is intended that under the general power to prescribe transitional arrangements, the Secretary of State will prescribe that, until such time as the Scottish Parliament enacts its own legislation for handling private legislation, procedures mirroring those in the Private Legislation Procedure (Scotland) Act 1936 will apply to private legislation promoted on devolved matters, except that, where there are references to the UK Parliament, these should be interpreted as meaning the Scottish Parliament and references to the Secretary of State should be interpreted as being to the Scottish Ministers. For the purpose of the Standing Orders, therefore, we have assumed that the 1936 procedures will apply. It is, therefore, proposed that until the Scottish Parliament makes its own legislation, the General Orders from Westminster should simply be replicated (and modified where necessary to take account of the Scottish Parliament) in the Scottish Parliament's Standing Orders.

Summary of Recommendations for Standing Orders

Standing Orders should:

- require draft Bills on Introduction to be accompanied by a memorandum explaining the consultative process undertaken and the degree of consensus reached, as well as

- the nature of the problem it is intended to address, and the strategic approach;

- the options considered, and why this particular option was chosen;

- the consultative process undertaken;

- the best estimated costs, benefits and financial implications;

- possibly, such other criteria as the impact on sustainable development, equal opportunities, implications for Islands communities, human rights and business cost compliance.

- provide that a Bill should not be introduced before the draft Bill is first referred to the Presiding Officer for his or her consideration.

- provide the form of the statement of a decision by the Presiding Officer on legislative competence; and for it to be published.

- provide that a Bill, once introduced, should be referred to the relevant Committee, which should consider and report on the general principles of the Bill to inform a debate and vote in Plenary. At this stage the Committee should also be able to comment on the Memorandum accompanying the Bill and to recommend whether further evidence should be taken to inform the next stage of consideration of the Bill.

- provide that following a debate and positive vote in Plenary on the principles of the Bill, the Bill should be referred to Committee for detailed consideration.

- provide that all MSPs should have the opportunity to propose amendments to a Bill, which should be considered in Committee.

- provide that Committee Stage should be able to be taken by the Plenary.

- provide that the Bill returned to Plenary from Committee should be accompanied by a report, explaining the Committee's reasons for the amendments.

- provide that further amendments, subject to tightly specified criteria should be allowed at this stage.

- provide that for the final vote to accept or reject a Bill, a quorum of Members, equivalent to at least 25% of the total number of seats in the Parliament should be required to vote. A simple majority of those voting would be required for a Bill to be amended.

- provide for expedited procedures for Bills which the Parliament agrees are emergency Bills.

- provide that Committees should be able to conduct inquiries, take evidence and report to the Parliament with recommendations for legislation.

- make provision for the Parliament, in Plenary, to adopt or reject the Report.

- provide that if the Committee's proposals for legislation are accepted, and the Executive does not indicate that it will bring forward such legislation, the Committee Convener should be authorised to instruct the preparation of a Bill on behalf of the Committee.

- provide that individual Members should be entitled to submit written proposals for legislation to the Presiding Officer. Such proposals should be brought before the Plenary if either they could secure the support of a minimum number of MSPs (perhaps 10% of the total), or by submitting them to the relevant subject Committee which should then have a discretionary competence to initiate an inquiry on the need for such legislation and to report to the Scottish Parliament.

- make provision for signifying Queen's Consent when necessary.

- require all subordinate legislation from the Executive which is required to be laid in the Parliament, to be sent both to the relevant subject Committee and to the Delegated Legislation Committee.

- in the case of private legislation, replicate the relevant General Orders at Westminster (with appropriate modifications).

COMMITTEE BILLS

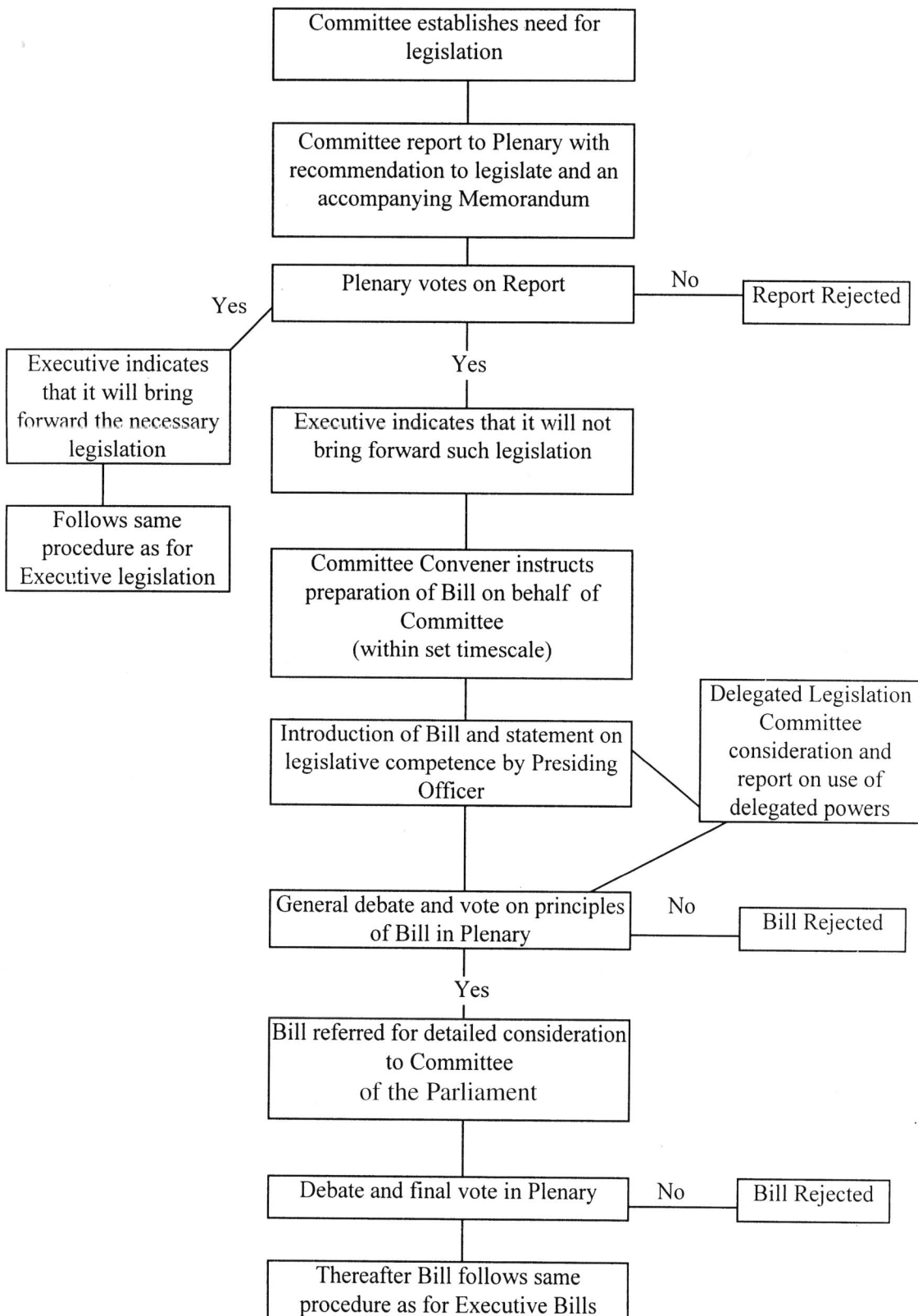

EXECUTIVE BILLS

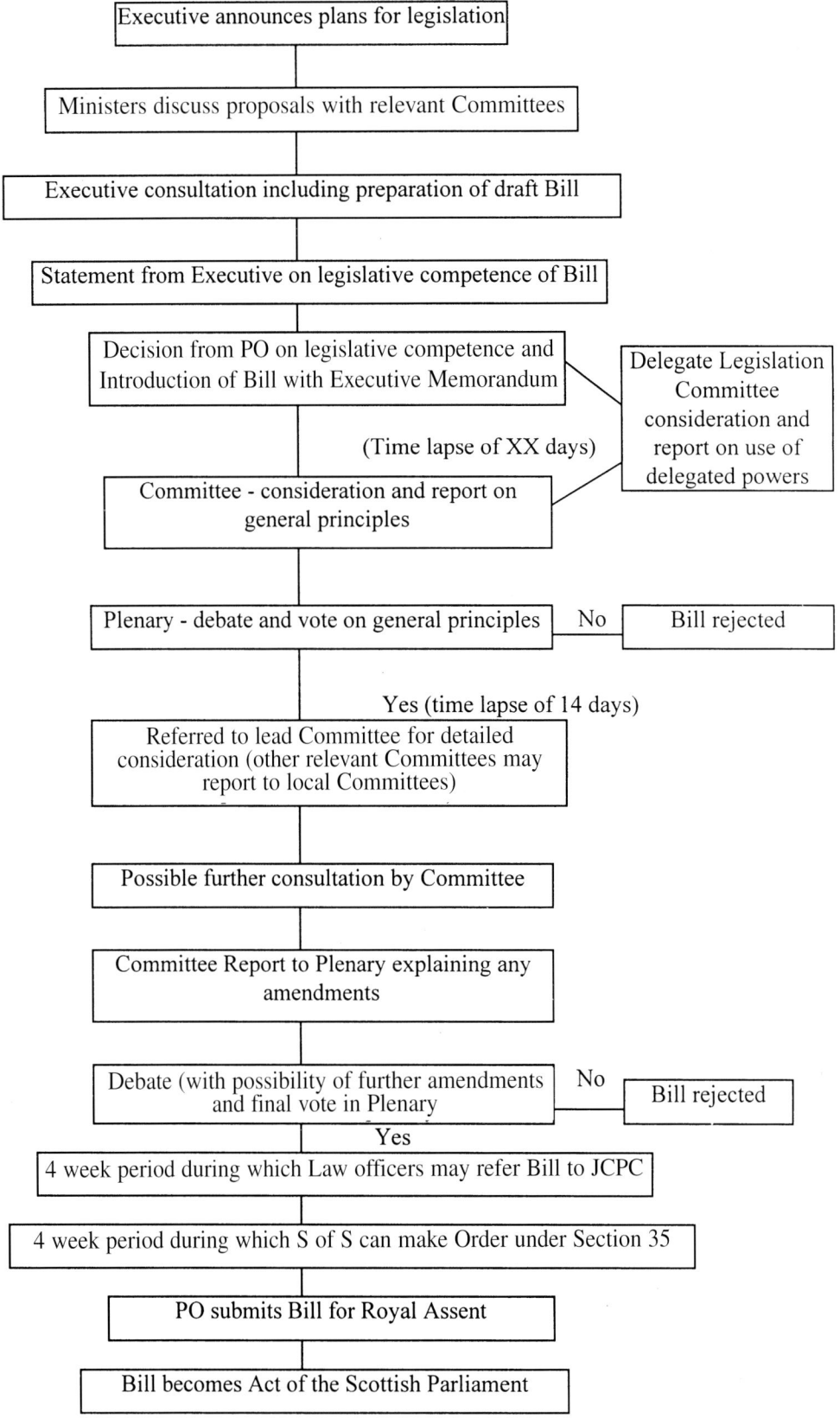

MEMBERS' BILLS

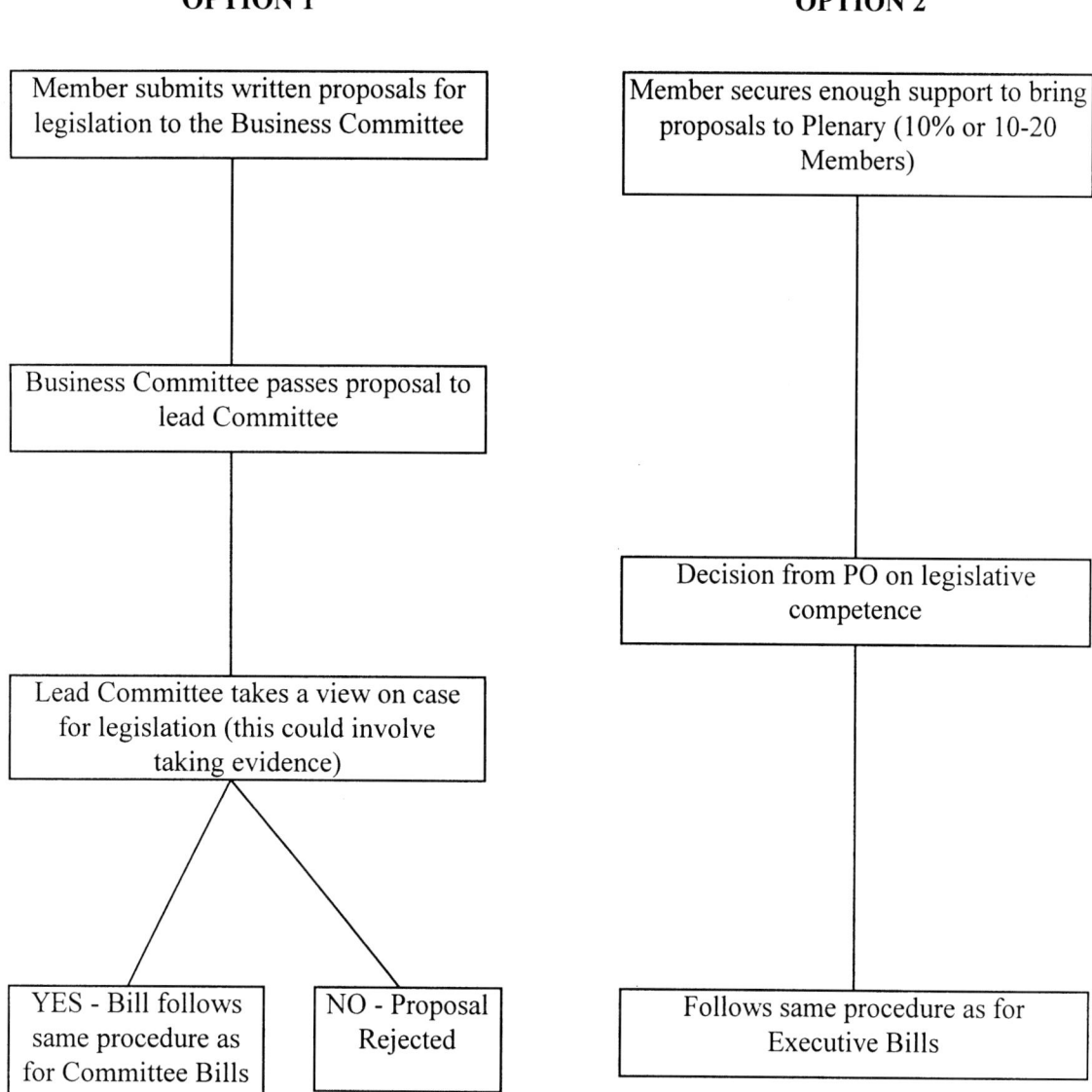

OPTION 1

Member submits written proposals for legislation to the Business Committee

Business Committee passes proposal to lead Committee

Lead Committee takes a view on case for legislation (this could involve taking evidence)

YES - Bill follows same procedure as for Committee Bills

NO - Proposal Rejected

OPTION 2

Member secures enough support to bring proposals to Plenary (10% or 10-20 Members)

Decision from PO on legislative competence

Follows same procedure as for Executive Bills

SECTION 3.6:

ACCESS AND INFORMATION

Introduction

1. We have already set out in section 2 a number of proposals aimed at meeting our third key principle, that the Scottish Parliament should be accessible, open, responsive, and develop procedures which make possible a participative approach to the development, consideration and scrutiny of policy and legislation. The principle of accessibility permeates our report, and is addressed in our recommendations on Committees (section 3.2), Parliamentary business (section 3.3), accountability (section 3.4) and the legislative process (section 3.5). This section sets out our recommendations on remaining access-related issues, including whether proceedings of the Parliament should be in public, the exclusion of individuals, public petitions, information and communications technologies.

Proceedings of the Parliament

2. Schedule 3, paragraph 3 of the Scotland Act requires Standing Orders to include provision requiring the proceedings of the Parliament to be held in public, and allows the Standing Orders to make provision for the circumstances under which proceedings of the Parliament may be closed to the public. It also allows Standing Orders to make provision as to the conditions to be complied with by any member of the public attending proceedings of the Parliament, including provision for excluding from the proceedings any member of the public who does not comply with these conditions.

3. We considered 2 separate issues: whether sessions in Plenary and in Committee should be public or private and, where such sessions are public, under what circumstances individuals may be excluded. In our deliberations we kept in mind our key principles relating to openness, accessibility and equal opportunities.

4. We recommend that Standing Orders should provide for all Plenary proceedings to be conducted in public. Different arrangements need to be put in place for Committees. The assumption is that Committees should normally meet in public. We recognise, however, that they will need the power to meet in private. However, against the background of the general principle of openness, Committees should keep the number of times they meet in private to a minimum. Standing Orders should authorise Committees to meet in private only with the agreement of a majority of the Committee members present. While this may at first appear to run counter to the principle of openness, we believe it is necessary to balance the need for openness with the nature of business and operational needs of the Parliament.

5. We recognise that it would be normal for Committees to meet in private to discuss approaches to business (for example, to evidence taking) and to consider, for example, how reports might be drawn up. Most Parliaments recognise the need for Committee meetings of this sort to be held in private. This would be preferable to the alternative situation, where the complete openness of all Committee proceedings could lead to genuine discussion taking place outside the official Committee proceedings.

REPORT OF THE CONSULTATIVE STEERING GROUP

6. However, we also propose that in addition Standing Orders should require Committees to produce regular say annual reports to the Parliament detailing the number of times the Committee has chosen to meet privately. These reports would be subject to Parliamentary scrutiny. This, coupled with the background of an open and accessible Parliament, should ensure that closed Committee sessions are the exception rather than the norm.

Exceptions

7. The only situation where this should not be the case should be in the consideration of legislation, where we propose that all Committee proceedings should be public.

8. We also propose that the Business Committee should always meet in private.

9. We also considered whether the Standards Committee should meet in private. While the business of the Standards Committee is of public interest, allegations of misconduct, which might eventually prove unfounded, could damage an MSP's reputation and consideration of such allegations might be held in private although conclusions would eventually become public in a Committee Report. We recommend that the Standards Committee should be able to meet in private where a majority of those Committee Members present felt it was necessary.

Reporting of Proceedings

10. If Committees are to meet in private, for example to discuss reports and make investigations, we propose that there should not be verbatim reporting of such proceedings, as that would remove the justification for the Committee meeting in private in the first place. Nevertheless, the conclusion of their deliberations must be made public. In practice, this would mean that reports of detailed discussions would not be available, but a note of final decisions should become public (perhaps in the form of a Committee report).

Exclusion of particular individuals

11. There are certain conditions under which it is proposed that members of the public should be excluded:

  - if drunk or under the influence of drugs;

  - if abusive;

  - if indulging in behaviour disruptive to the proceedings (such as speaking loudly, throwing things or using intrusive electronic equipment).

12. We recommend that the Presiding Officer should be given a general power to exclude individuals from the public gallery, when the individual has met one of these conditions. Conveners should be given the same powers in respect of Committees.

Public Petitions

Principles

13. It is an important principle that the Scottish people should be able to petition the Parliament directly.

14.   Against the background of our key principles of openness and accessibility, equal opportunities, accountability and sharing the power, we believe that any system adopted for public petitions should satisfy the following criteria:

-   public petitions should be encouraged by the Parliament;

-   any member of the public should be able to petition the Parliament;

-   there should be clear and simple rules as to form and content;

-   it should be clear to petitioners how and to whom petitions should be submitted;

-   there should be clear expectations of how petitions will be handled, the form of response which can be expected and the time in which such a response can be expected; and

-   all petitions and responses should be in the public domain.

Criteria for acceptance

15.   We considered the criteria to be used to determine whether a petition to the Scottish Parliament can be accepted. We concluded that the Parliament should accept all petitions for which the remedy sought would be within the competence of the Scottish Parliament.

Issues

16.   We also considered whether there should be a minimum level of support which a petition should enjoy for there to be an automatic obligation on the Parliament to take a certain course of action. This approach is used by a number of other Parliaments we looked at.   However a set number of signatures to a petition requiring action by the Parliament might act against individuals or organisations based in more remote areas. For example, it could be much easier to collect 10,000 signatures in Glasgow than in a remote Highland village. Further, a rule requiring action but only where the petition has a minimum number of signatures would only make sense in practice if there were procedures for verifying the authenticity of purported signatures and any such procedure might prove unduly time consuming and difficult to operate. We recommend that the action taken by the Parliament on a particular petition should be dependent on a wide assessment of the strength and depth of support it enjoys, and not only on the number of signatures the petition has.

Presentation to the Parliament and Action to be Taken

17.   Any member of the public should be able to present a written petition either to one of their MSPs or directly to Parliament.

18.   All petitions should be passed in the first instance to a Committee for Petitions whose first task should be to decide whether the remedy sought by the petitioner fell within the competence of the Parliament. The Committee should also be required to acknowledge receipt of all petitions within a prescribed time limit, informing the petitioners of the action and/or decisions the Committee has taken. The Committee should be given a range of options in dealing with petitions, for example :

- no action if the remedy sought fell outwith the competence of the Parliament;

- forward the petition, along with a brief report outlining the Committee's views, to the Scottish Executive for information or consideration;

- forward the petition to relevant national/regional authorities for information or consideration;

- refer the petition to the relevant subject Committee within the Parliament for information, consideration or action; and

- prepare a report on the petition to be submitted to the Plenary for consideration and/or debate.

Information and Communications Technologies

19. We were informed by the work of the Expert Panel on Information and Communications Technologies, whose report has been published separately (ISBN No. 0 7480 7252 7).

20. We believe that the use of ICT is not an end in itself. To be worthwhile, it must help materially and measurably the achievement of the overall objectives for the Parliament. In our discussions, we found that objectives for ICT generally fall under 2 headings - promoting Parliamentary efficiency through supporting modern ways of working with well-designed information technology; and promoting openness, accountability and democratic participation in Scotland by using technology to make information about the Parliament and its work available to everyone. Provision of ICT must be set in the context of the Parliament's business, so that its success can be measured against the degree to which it helps to meet the objectives of the organisation.

21. We recommend that the following principles should apply to ICT in the Parliament:

- it should be innovative;

- it should allow the Parliament to develop its use of ICT in a planned and coherent way;

- it should seize the opportunities which modern, well-designed information systems offer for improving openness, accessibility and responsiveness to the people of Scotland;

- it should aspire to be an example of best practice in Parliamentary information systems, both in terms of external communications and internal efficiency;

- it should lay the basis for delivering the business of the Parliament efficiently and effectively.

22. We therefore urge that ICT in the Parliament should:

- support the business of the Parliament, through the provision of appropriate information systems and facilities which meet the needs of MSPs, their support staff and Parliamentary staff;

- support MSPs, their support staff and the staff of the Parliament regardless of their physical location;

- support on-line access by the public to:

  - information about the business of the Parliament

  - information about MSPs

  - information about the Parliament's constitution and history

- support communications with:

  - national elected bodies at Westminster, in Wales and in Northern Ireland

  - other elected bodies, including local authorities and the EU

  - the public, businesses and the voluntary sector

  - Government Departments, Agencies and organisations

- provide consistent, timely, accurate and accessible information, presented attractively and creatively;

- use up-to-date, reliable technology which conforms to widely adopted industry standards;

- be capable of responding to changing demands from MSPs, their support staff, staff of the Parliament and the public.

23.   We endorse the detailed recommendations of the Expert Panel on ICT.

Summary of Recommendations for Standing Orders

Standing Orders should provide:

- that all Plenary proceedings should be conducted in public.

- that Committees should have the power to meet in private, only with the agreement of the majority of Committee members present.

- that Committees should produce regular reports to the Parliament detailing the number of times the Committee has chosen to meet privately.

- when legislation is under consideration, all Committee meetings should be public.

- that the Business Committee should always meet in private.

- that members of the public may be excluded if drunk or under the influence of drugs; if abusive; if indulging in disruptive behaviour.

- that the Parliament should accept all petitions for which the remedy sought would be within the competence of the Parliament.

- that all petitions should be passed in the first instance to a Committee for Petitions.

- that the Committee should be required to acknowledge receipt of all petitions within the prescribed time limit, informing the petitioners of the actions and/or decisions the Committee had taken.

- that the Committee should be given a range of options for dealing with petitions for example:

  - no action if the remedy sought fell outwith the competence of the Parliament;

  - forward the petition, along with a brief report outlining the Committee's views, to the Scottish Executive for information or consideration;

  - forward the petition to relevant national/regional authorities for information or consideration;

  - refer the petition to the relevant subject Committee within the Parliament for information, consideration or action; and

  - prepare a report on the petition to be submitted to the Plenary for consideration and/or debate.

NEXT STEPS

1.   There remains a significant amount of work to be done to ensure that the principles and recommendations set out in this report are given effect to and that the Scottish Parliament is able to begin its operations smoothly and effectively.

Standing Orders

2.   One of the main tasks will be for the Secretary of State to prepare a set of Standing Orders for the Parliament, to be prescribed by him through secondary legislation made under the Scotland Act 1998. We recommend that our proposals should form the basis of those Standing Orders. We will meet early in 1999 to comment and advise on the draft Standing Orders.

Code of Conduct Working Group and Media Issues Panel

3.   This report already includes recommendations on the principles which should form the basis for any Code of Conduct for MSPs. However, further work remains to be done on the detail of that Code. The Code of Conduct Working Group will report early in 1999 and will make recommendations on a range of issues concerning the proper conduct of MSPs, including rules governing the registration and declaration of Members' interests, together with recommendations on the regulation of lobbying activities.

4.   The Media Issues Panel will also report in the spring, with recommendations on the relationship between the Parliament and the media, how the Parliament might present itself through the media, how the media should conduct itself while covering the Parliament and terms on which members of the Scottish Administration and staff should have contact with and speak to the media.

5.   We will review and consider the reports of these groups, to inform a supplementary CSG report, to be published in March 1999.

Other Issues

6.   Other issues which will be taken forward include a substantial awareness raising information campaign in advance of the first elections to the Parliament; the development of curriculum material for civic education; the plans for the opening ceremony; the physical arrangements for the Parliament; the implementation of the recommendations of the Expert Panel on ICT, including the development of a Parliamentary web-site; the recruitment and training of the staff of the Parliament; the training of MSPs; and the development of new structures in civic society. We will have a continuing interest in reviewing progress on these issues.

Timetable for the First Meetings of the Parliament

7.   We expect that the Secretary of State will prescribe by the end of March 1999 the Standing Orders that will govern the first meetings of the Scottish Parliament.

8.   The Secretary of State has announced his intention that the elections to the Scottish Parliament should be held on 6 May 1999.

9.   Thereafter it is expected that it will take one or two days after the elections to verify all the returns, to provide the authority required to recognise Members of the Scottish Parliament. During the week immediately following the elections there will also be a number of routine issues to be attended to, such as the allocation of MSPs' offices, security passes etc.

10.   It is likely therefore that the first meeting of the Parliament will take place around one week after the elections. The date, time and place will be prescribed by the Secretary of State early in 1999.

11.   The first business will be the taking of the oath by MSPs. (Until they have taken the oath, MSPs are unable to participate in proceedings of the Parliament.) This would be followed by the election of the Presiding Officer and Deputy Presiding Officers.

12.   The Scotland Act allows 28 days from the date of the elections for the Parliament to nominate the First Minister. It is hoped however that he or she could be nominated within the first 14 days after the elections. The first business of the second meeting might be the nomination of the First Minister. The First Minister will have to be appointed by The Queen before he or she can seek the Parliament's approval of the choice of Scottish Ministers and junior Scottish Ministers. The form and shape of the Scottish Executive and the Scottish Administration is therefore likely to emerge in the course of May.

13.   In the first few weeks of its life the Parliament will need to authorise and appoint Members to the various Committees which it intends to establish or which are prescribed in Standing Orders. It is expected that the Business Committee will begin to make recommendations to the Parliament on the establishment of Committees during this period. The Committees may wish to meet for an initial discussion of the work they wish to undertake over the year ahead.

14.   Four MSPs will have to be appointed to the Scottish Parliamentary Corporate Body. If the Parliament fails to nominate 4 candidates within one month of the elections, the Presiding Officer will be able to appoint Members.

15.   During the early weeks of the Parliament, a programme of information and training for MSPs will continue. The period between the elections and the Parliament assuming its full powers will provide a valuable opportunity for MSPs to familiarise themselves with the working arrangements of the Parliament.

16.   Certain items of subordinate legislation arising from the Scotland Act 1998 and relating to the transfer of power to the Scottish Parliament will need to be considered and approved during June.

17.   On 1 July 1999 the Parliament will be given its full legislative powers, functions will be transferred to the Scottish Executive and the formal opening ceremony will be held.

LIST OF ANNEXES

Annex A: Remits and membership of Expert Panels and Working Groups
Annex B: Research
Annex C: CSG consultation paper
Annex D: Analysis of written responses to the consultation exercise
Annex E: Analysis of points raised in open forums
Annex F: Draft Information Strategy for the Scottish Parliament
Annex G: Consultation mechanisms
Annex H: Mainstreaming Equal Opportunities
Annex I: Financial Issues Advisory Group: Summary of Recommendations
Annex J: Expert Panel on Information and Communications Technologies: Summary of Recommendations by the sub-group on Democratic Participation

ANNEX A

EXPERT PANELS AND WORKING GROUPS

Expert Panel on Procedures and Standing Orders in the Scottish Parliament

Membership

The members of the Group are:

Mr Robert Gordon, The Scottish Office, Head of Constitution Group (Chair)

Ms Morag Alexander, Director, Equal Opportunities Commission

Professor St John Bates, Visiting Professor of Law, University of Strathclyde and Clerk to the Isle of Man Tynwald

Mr Francis Jacobs, Secretariat, European Parliament

Ms Lynne MacMillan, formerly Head of Legal Policy, Scottish Consumer Council

Professor David McCrone, Unit for the Study of Government in Scotland, University of Edinburgh

Mr Bill McKay CB, Clerk to the House of Commons

Mr David Millar OBE, Co-author of the Crick-Millar draft Standing Orders for a Scottish Parliament

Professor Alan Miller, Director, Scottish Human Rights Centre

Ms Esther Roberton, Consultative Steering Group on the Scottish Parliament

Mr Martin Sime, Director, Scottish Council for Voluntary Organisations

Mr Douglas Sinclair, Chief Executive, Convention of Scottish Local Authorities

Remit

The remit for the Panel is:

- to assist The Scottish Office with the development and assessment of policy options relating to the proceedings, working methods and operation of the Scottish Parliament, for consideration by CSG;

- to assist in the development of detailed proposals for the rules of procedure and Standing Orders which the Parliament might be asked to adopt, against the background of the deliberations of CSG and the key principles endorsed by CSG;

- in both of the above, to take into account the evidence gathered by CSG;

- to assist in the preparation of a draft report to the Secretary of State by the end of 1998, to inform the preparation of draft Standing Orders.

Financial Issues Advisory Group

Membership

The members of the Financial Issues Advisory Group are:

Mr John Graham, The Scottish Office, Principal Finance Officer (Chair) (until end May 1997)

Dr Peter Collings, The Scottish Office, Principal Finance Officer (Chair) (from 1 June 1997)

Mr Robert Black, Controller of Audit, Accounts Commission

Mr Andrew Edwards CB, Financial Consultant and former Deputy Secretary at the Treasury

Mrs Margaret Ford, head of the Eglinton Management School and Chairman of Lothian Health Board

Professor David Heald, Aberdeen University

Miss Eileen Mackay CB, member of Commission on Local Government and the Scottish Parliament and former PFO, The Scottish Office

Ms Shelagh Mackay, Director of Finance, Shepherd and Wedderburn

Mr Miller McLean, Group Secretary, Royal Bank of Scotland

Mr Martin Pfleger, Assistant Auditor General, National Audit Office

Professor John Sizer, Chief Executive, Scottish Higher Education Funding Council

Mr Ian Smith, Chief Executive, Dumfries and Galloway Council

Dr Joan Stringer, Principal, Queen Margaret College and member of the Consultative Steering Group

Mr Alf Young, Deputy Editor of the Herald

Remit

The remit of FIAG is:

To assist The Scottish Office in developing for consideration by the Consultative Steering Group (CSG), proposals for the rules, procedures, standing orders and legislation which the

Scottish Parliament might be invited to adopt for handling financial issues, taking account of the deliberations of the CSG and contributing to the draft report which the CSG is to submit to the Secretary of State by the end of 1998 to inform the preparation of draft Standing Orders.

Expert Panel on Information and Communication Technologies

Membership

The membership of the Expert Panel on Information and Communications Technologies is:

Mr Alistair Brown, The Scottish Office, Director of Administrative Services (Chair)

Mr Alistair Baker, Microsoft Corporation

Mr Robert Beattie MBE, Chair of Edinburgh Telematics Partnership and Community Investment Manager, IBM Scotland

Mrs Lesley Beddie, Professor of Computing, Napier University

Mr Peter Black, Network Service Adviser, Scottish Telecom

Mr Peter Dixon, Oracle Corporation

Mr Nic Hopkins, Technical Director, Central Computers and Telecommunications Agency (CCTA)

Ms Derdre Hutton, Consultative Steering Group on the Scottish Parliament

Mr Paul Grice, The Scottish Office, Constitution Group

Mr Dik McFarlane, General Manager, Office of the Director, BT Scotland

Dr Ann Mathieson OBE, Keeper, National Library for Scotland

Mr Alan Nairn, Secretary, Society of IT Managers (Scotland) and Director of Information Systems, Perth & Kinross Council

Mr Matthew O'Connor, Director of Business Services, Telewest Communications

Mrs Jane Wainwright, Director of Information Systems, House of Commons Library

Ms Ann Weatherstone, Assistant Director of Strategic Planning at Clydesdale Bank, Glasgow

Remit

The panel will provide advice to The Scottish Office on how the Parliament might use technology to:

- promote internal efficiency and innovative ways of working;

- provide information about its proceedings and its work to the widest possible audience in the most accessible way;

- make it as easy as possible for the Parliament and individual MSPs to exchange information with external organisations and the public;

- encourage democratic participation and involvement.

As part of its work, the panel will consider the proposals and recommendations made by the Advisory Committee on Telematics for the Scottish Parliament, as set out in their report of June 1997.

The panel is expected to produce practical proposals together with resource estimates and a summary of the benefits which are expected to flow from them. The proposals should be prioritised, should take into account the fact that the Parliament will meet in temporary accommodation for around 2 years from 1999, and should be suitable for implementation in phases.

The panel should also provide advice to The Scottish Office on information and communications technology in the context of wider consideration of the Parliament's ways of working. The panel should be able to consult on its proposals before bringing these forward to the Consultative Steering Group, including consultation with potential users of Parliamentary information.

The panel is expected to work closely with other expert panels set up to advise The Scottish Office. It is expected to provide draft proposals for discussion with the Consultative Steering Group to a timetable to be agreed with the Group, but it should aim to complete the bulk of its work in 1998.

Code of Conduct Working Group

Membership

The membership of the Group is:

Mr John Ewing, The Scottish Office, Constitutional Policy Division (Chair)

Rev Maxwell Craig, nominated by Action of Churches Together in Scotland

Mr John F de W Duvoisin, nominated by the Institute of Chartered Accountants of Scotland

Mr Martyn Evans, Chief Executive Officer, Scottish Consumer Council

Dr Brian D Keighley, nominated by the British Medical Association

Professor Sheila McLean, Dept. of Law and Ethics in Medicine, Glasgow University

Professor Alan Miller, EXPSO (and Scottish Human Rights Centre)

Mr John Murray, nominated by the Scottish Daily Newspaper Society

Miss Jane Ryder, nominated by the Law Society of Scotland

Mr Douglas Sinclair, nominated by COSLA (also a member of EXPSO)

Canon Kenyon Wright, Consultative Steering Group

Remit

The remit of the group is:

- to assist The Scottish Office in developing for consideration by the Consultative Steering Group on the Scottish Parliament (CSG) proposals for a Code of Conduct for MSPs which the Scottish Parliament might be invited to adopt;

- to consider and provide advice to officials on what form of regulation if any might be recommended to the Scottish Parliament in respect of lobbying activities;

- in carrying out 1 and 2 to consider the views of CSG as well as existing UK Ministerial and Civil Service Codes, the current proposals for local government and the practice in other relevant organisations.

Media Issues Expert Panel

Membership

Mr Robert Gordon, The Scottish Office, Head of Constitution Group (Chair)

Ms Val Atkinson, Deputy Head of News and Current Affairs, BBC Scotland

Ms Fiona Ballantyne, Director, Network Scotland

Mrs Lesley Beddie, Professor of Computing, Napier University

Mr Martyn Evans, Chief Executive Officer, Scottish Consumer Council

Mr Kenny Farquharson, Spokesperson, Scottish Parliamentary Press Association

Ms Frances Horsburgh, Political Correspondent, The Herald

Ms Harriet Jones, Head of News, Scot FM

Mr John Penman, Assistant Editor, Daily Record

Mr George Reid, Consultative Steering Group

Mr John Scott, Editor, Evening Times

Mr Mark Smith, Senior Producer, Scottish Television

Mr Ramsay Smith, Editor, Scottish Daily Mail

Mr Brian Taylor, Political Editor, BBC Scotland

Remit

The remit of the Expert Panel is:

To advise on how the Parliament and the media should relate to each other, how the Parliament will present itself through the media, how the media will conduct itself while covering the Parliament and on the terms on which MSPs, including members and staff of the administration, have contact with and speak to the media.

ANNEX B

LIST OF RESEARCH COMMISSIONED BY CSG

ISBN No

SCEC Report: 'Have your say!' Consultation with Young People on Local Government and The Scottish Parliament August 1998 – Report.

07480 72403

The Constitution Unit: Checks and Balances in Single Chamber Parliaments: A Comparative Study.

07480 72497

The Constitution Unit: Single Chamber Parliaments: A Comparative Study (Stage Two).

07480 72535

Centre for Scottish Public Policy: Parliamentary Practices in Devolved Parliaments.

07480 72454

Report from Focus Groups by The Scottish Consumer Council and Rural Forum Scotland: Public Consultation on the Operation of The Scottish Parliament.

07480 72489

Glasgow Caledonian University: Telematics and the Scottish Parliament: Transferable Democratic Innovations.

07480 72446

The University of Edinburgh: 'Mainstreaming' Equal Opportunities.

07480 72411

The University of Edinburgh: Citizen Participation and Social Partnerships: Involving Civil Society in the Work of Parliaments.

07480 7242X

The University of Edinburgh: Summary of Devolved Parliaments in the European Union.

07480 7239X

ANNEX C

CSG CONSULTATION PAPER

YOUR VIEWS ON HOW THE SCOTTISH PARLIAMENT SHOULD WORK

Background

The Consultative Steering Group on the Scottish Parliament has agreed a number of key principles against which the Group will consider issues relating to the operation of the Scottish Parliament. These are:

- the Scottish Parliament should embody and reflect the sharing of power between the people of Scotland, the legislators and the Scottish Executive;

- the Scottish Executive should be accountable to the Scottish Parliament and the Parliament and Executive should be accountable to the people of Scotland;

- the Scottish Parliament should be accessible, open, responsive and develop procedures which make possible a participative approach to the development, consideration and scrutiny of policy and legislation;

- the Scottish Parliament in its operation and its appointments should recognise the need to promote equal opportunities for all.

The Consultative Steering Group (CSG) invites you to consider the following questions which arise from these key principles in responding to this consultation exercise. However, your views on any other aspect of the working arrangements of the Parliament would be welcome.

SHARING THE POWER

- How can the Parliament best organise its work to take the views of the public into account, both in its initial organisation and its ongoing work?

- What arrangements should there be for involving civic society, women's groups, people from ethnic minority communities, people with disabilities, business and the general public (taking account of resource implications)?

- How might the Parliament reach those groups not normally involved in the political process?

- What sort of ethos should Parliament develop?

- How might Parliament's ethos be reflected in the Parliament's traditions and ceremonies?

ACCOUNTABILITY

MSPs

- How might MSPs be made accountable to the electorate other than through the election process?

- Should the MSP provide regular feedback to the electorate on the work of the Parliament and what form could this take?

- Should there be a code of conduct for MSPs and if so what should it cover?

- How might equal opportunities be addressed in such a code of conduct?

- What arrangements should be made for the registration of MSPs' interests?

Should there be regulation of the process of lobbying of MSPs?

Scottish Executive

- Taking the current Westminster arrangements as a starting point, would you like to see the Scottish Ministers accounting to the Parliament in different ways?

ACCESSIBLE, OPEN, RESPONSIVE

The Design Brief is intended to make the Parliament physically accessible. The culture of the Parliament should also be accessible.

- What steps might the Parliament take to develop an accessible culture?

- How can it make its working practices transparent and understandable?

- How should it ensure that people have information about the Parliament,?

- Should there be special arrangements put in place for schools?

- Should there be special arrangements for other sectors of Scottish society?

Committees are an important part of most Parliaments including Westminster - there specific Select Committees investigate the work of particular Government Departments and separate Standing Committees scrutinise legislation. The White Paper said that the Government expected Committees to play an important part in carrying out the Scottish Parliament's business.

- What Committee structure should the Parliament create?

- Should there be separate select and standing Committees or should there be single Committees investigating the work of government departments and scrutinising legislation?

- Should there be Committees reflecting the structure of The Scottish Office or should they cut across the work of Departments?

- How might equal opportunities issues be addressed in the work of Committees?

- How should membership of Committees be decided?

- How should Committees initiate legislation?

- What role might non-MSPs play in Committees?

The Parliament will be responsible for making laws for Scotland on subjects which are within its legislative competence. At present, Bills are not formally scrutinised until they are introduced into the Westminster Parliament (although the policy may have been the subject of a Government consultative paper). CSG believes that proposals for the Scottish Parliament legislation should be the subject of consultation, discussion and scrutiny before formal introduction.

- How might such pre-legislative scrutiny be undertaken?

- How might the views of interest groups and the impact of new policies on them be taken into account before and during the legislative process?

- What information should the Parliament take into account when considering proposals (eg financial implications, equal opportunities implications, environmental impact, implications for business)?

- How can the Parliament ensure that legislation is properly considered?

- Should existing legislation be reviewed and if so how? What factors might be taken into account (eg financial implications, equal opportunities implications, environmental impact, implications for business)?

The Parliament should operate as efficiently as possible, and the working practices it adopts should help achieve this:

- Should there be electronic voting?

- How can it make the best use of Information Technology, the Internet, electronic mail?

- What other Best Practice could the Parliament draw on?

EQUAL OPPORTUNITIES

The Scottish Parliament is likely to keep normal business hours and take Scottish school holidays:

- What else should it take into account to ensure that the Parliament is open to all?

- What other practices could be adopted to promote equal opportunities?

- How might the language and other practices of the Parliament be inclusive/non-discriminatory?

ANNEX D

CONSULTATIVE STEERING GROUP ON THE SCOTTISH PARLIAMENT:

ANALYSIS TO THE RESPONSES TO THE CONSULTATION DOCUMENT ON THE OPERATION OF THE SCOTTISH PARLIAMENT

1. Appendix A to this Annex lists all the responses to the consultation exercise received by 31 July. The Appendix also provides a breakdown of response by:

- type of organisation/individual;

- format of submission (ie letter or e.mail);

A number of respondents requested that their submissions be kept confidential. Their names have not been included in Appendix A and, unlike other submissions, they are not available for public viewing in St Andrews House Library. However the main points realised in confidential submissions have been taken into account in this analysis.

Methodology

2. A qualitative, rather than a quantitative approach was used in the analysis of the responses. This was felt to be generally more appropriate as it allowed subtle distinctions between different standpoints to be noted. It also allowed for the views of particular relevant organisations to be drawn out (although the views of all organisations and individuals have been taken into account). Direct quotes and attributions have been used to indicate expressed viewpoints where these are seen to be representative, and have in most cases been backed up by further examples.

Other issues

3. The consultation document invited responses on many aspect of the working arrangements of the new Parliament. Many respondents, however, included in their submissions details of their opinions, aspirations and comments on the policies which they considered the Scottish Parliament should adopt. This is of course beyond the remit of the CSG. Where possible, such comments have been passed on to the Division within the Scottish Office with policy responsibility for that area.

Analysis

4. The analysis of responses which follows reflects the order of questions in the consultation document. Questions have been combined where responses largely covered

more than one question. At the same time, many recipients did not follow the question format suggested in the consultation document, and responses often cross more than one heading (for example, the issue of the role of non MSPs in Committees has been included under the *Accessibility/Openness/Participation* heading, but was discussed by many respondees under the topic of *Sharing the Power*.) Cross-references to other headings have been included as far as possible.

Sharing the Power

5. *How can the Parliament best organise its work to take the views of the public into account, both in its initial organisation and its ongoing work?*

6. *What arrangements should there be for involving civic society, women's groups, people from ethnic minority communities, people with disabilities, business and the general public (taking account of resource implications)?*

6.1   Recipients were in general very supportive of any mechanisms which could be found to involve the public, civic society and representative groups in the work of the Parliament, and a variety of imaginative methods for doing so were suggested.   In particular, voluntary organisations and interest groups were particularly keen to see that formal systems were put in place to allow them to speak as representatives of their constituent groups. Many voluntary organisations in particular (for example, Fair Play) suggested that the Parliament should set up a database of registered consultees who would automatically be approached on any relevant issues. Voluntary organisations were very keen to see that a distinctive role was given to them as acting as a conduit between government and civic society. For example, the Royal Society for the Protection of Birds stressed that non-Governmental Organisations already involved a wide variety of the population who felt that such interest groups more accurately reflected their concerns than the traditional political parties. It would therefore be sensible to use such NGOs and their existing networks (and the basic consultation mechanisms already in place) to encourage greater consultation with, and participation by, the public in the political process.   At the same time, the Equal Opportunities Commission stressed the need for machinery to be put in place which would ensure fair representation for minority groups in the consultation process.

6.2   The need for early consultation was seen as a key to improving the existing opportunities for involvement of civic society in the decision making process. Many recipients felt that current Scottish Office arrangements for consultation did not allow sufficient time for response - a minimum period of 12 weeks was suggested by many groups as allowing them sufficient time to collate responses from the variety of sources which they needed to consult to be sure of a representative response.

6.3   Local Government representatives also brought forward a distinct view that the existing infrastructure of local government could be used as an interface between Parliament and the public, as it provided a layer of governance more accessible to the person on the street. For example, North Lanarkshire Council considered that a partnership approach between the new Parliament and the local authorities would have the advantage of allowing for local government to be used as a means of collecting public opinion.

6.4   Local authorities were also vociferous in claiming particular rights for councils, translated into statutory duties for the Parliament: West Lothian Council, for example, suggested that the Parliament should be statutorily obliged to consult local government on relevant issues.

6.5   Councils (and others) also brought forward suggestions for the transfer of local authority good practice to the work of the Parliament in encouraging maximum participation. Such practice included: the use of citizens' juries to gauge public opinion; the dissemination of material via the Internet, and the co-option of non elected members onto Committees (this issue will be returned to under the heading of Accessibility).

6.6   Other proposals for involving the public in the workings of the Parliament which featured regularly in responses were:

- the provision of a well-resourced Public Information Service which would welcome visitors to the Parliament and explain its operations;

- the provision of a large public gallery open at all times;

- allowing Committees to travel around the country;

- making provision for groups and individuals to communicate with the Parliament and its MSPs by non-traditional means (for example video presentations), especially when these groups and individuals were located in more remote areas;

- as much material on the Parliament in general, and its timetable, reporting of debates and so on, available in an easily digestible format on the Internet.

6.7   Many respondents answered these questions by considering what mechanisms could be used to involve representative groups in the pre-legislative consultation process, and how these could interact with the Committees of the Parliament. Because both the pre-legislative process and Committees come up in the section on Accessibility, these responses are considered in that context.

7. *How might the Parliament reach those groups not normally involved in the political process?*

7.1   In general, the suggestions being generated under this heading were similar to those for questions 8 and 9. At the same time, however, there was a distinct recognition (especially from voluntary groups representing social excluded sections of the population) that new mechanisms needed to be found to encourage their integration into the decision-making process, thus avoiding consultation only with the "usual suspects". Age Concern Scotland, for example, believe that older people in themselves represent an excluded group whose expertise needs to be harnessed into the political process. They suggest that this may be done via non-traditional methods of consultation such as User Panels targeted at specific excluded groups.

7.2   At the same time, organisations representing the disabled and ethnic minorities stress that these groups' access to information on the Parliament is a key to the extent to which they are able to participate in the process. So, for example, the Royal National Institute for the Blind pointed out that the blind could only genuinely be involved in the consultation process if materials were made available in accessible formats (Braille, large print and so on) and if assistance was provided for them so they could reach the venues where consultation was taking place. In the same way, Grampian Racial Equality Council suggested that interpreters should be available as necessary at public consultation meetings.

7.3   Similarly, there was a recognition that access to information could act as a key to overcoming the cynicism of those not normally involved in the political process. WEA Scotland came up with this suggestion: *"Engaging groups not normally involved in the political process will require immediate recourse to a programme of education for all citizens. Courses would cover aspects of researching issues, developing negotiating skills, lobbying and campaigning skills as well as the matter of understanding the system of government that will be put in place".* The assumption here is that the Parliament will need to make funding available to such groups to help them disseminate information and educate excluded groups and individuals. Another suggestion made along the same lines was that the Parliament should consider the establishment of Democratic Centres across Scotland, drawing on South Africa's model of the Institute of Democracy.

7.4   BT Scotland, amongst others, broadened out this issue of reaching excluded groups and gave various examples of innovative ways in which those cut off from the political process perhaps by apathy or poverty could be encouraged to participate. They regard ICT as being at the heart of the democratic process, but recognise that it has to be used so that those without access to expensive computer technology are able to tap into it. They suggest, therefore, that the distribution of information via the Internet is complemented by a teletext information service and a Parliamentary call centre to deal with queries from the public. While other groups propose a dedicated digital TV channel showing the proceedings of the Parliament, BT suggest that easily digestible broadcasts, sparking people's interest in the Parliament, are shown in public venues such as shopping centres and sports venues.

7.5   The suggestion was also made, for example by the STUC Black Workers' Committee, that national and local forums of "social partners" could be set up to discuss public policy, and to integrate the voice of democratically accountable groups into the policy formulation process.

7.6   Finally, various groups (the Scottish Association for Mental Health among others) took up the Crick-Millar suggestion that the voices of individuals could be heard by the Parliament if they had an automatic right to trigger some form of Parliamentary process if the signatures of a minimum number of individuals could be gained (eg, the right to a Parliamentary debate on a particular subject if 10,000 signatures were collected, and so on). In a similar vein, Aberdeen City Council suggested that: "It should be possible for citizens and their organisations to demand that a Committee enquire into a particular community concern."

8.   *What sort of ethos should the Parliament develop?*

8.1   There was a great deal of agreement in response to this question, with nearly all respondees stating that the Parliament's ethos should be open and consensual, avoiding the Westminster style of confrontational and point-scoring politics. The Scottish Council of National Training Organisations summed this up by describing the desired ethos as that of a "People's Parliament". Responses showed a definite disillusionment with the Westminster style of politics. The British Federation of Women Graduates hope that the Parliament will be "a caring body whose members are free from the self-interest and sleaze that has been so much a feature of the Westminster Parliament in recent years". This view was echoed by representative groups, individuals and voluntary organisations. The Commission for Racial Equality and the Equal Opportunities Commission both expressed a hope that the ethos would be one which respected diversity, and in the same vein the Northern Joint Police Board stated that they sought a Parliament whose ethos would be sensitive to needs of the various parts of Scotland, and not focused narrowly on the central belt. The theme, therefore was one of inclusiveness.

9. *How might Parliament's ethos be reflected in the Parliament's traditions and ceremonies?*

9.1 Aspirations for the Parliament's traditions and ceremonies mirrored views about its ethos; respondees hoped to see simple ceremonies which would be inclusive, rather than alienating the public by their apparent irrelevance (as is thought to be the case at Westminster). As the Scottish Green Party said: **"Leave old-fashioned ceremonies behind - no old fashioned robes and long wigs to perpetuate the old elitist system".** Although the ceremonies would not be overly ornate or formal, respondees hoped that they would be dignified, thus indicating the significance of the Parliament. Some individuals and organisations (for example, the Law Society of Scotland) were keen to see some elements of pre-1707 Parliamentary traditions brought into the proceedings, but this view was not as popular as that which believed that the new Parliament should have completely modern traditions, possibly developing over time rather than being prescribed at the outset of the Parliament's life. According to the Campaign for a Scottish Parliament, *"Prestige should come from the quality of the work not pretension"*.

Accountability

10. *How might MSPs be made accountable to the electorate other than through the election process?*

11. *Should the MSP provide regular feedback to the electorate on the work of the Parliament and what form could this take?*

11.1 There was a general consensus amongst respondees from all sectors that it would be a positive step if MSPs were required to make themselves accountable to the electorate not only via the ballot box, but on a regular basis. The following suggestions for how this could be achieved were particularly popular:

- regular spot in local newspaper;

- regular publication of a constituency newsletter detailing latest activities;

- regular report on activities including statistical information such as attendance and voting records;

- regular local meetings with constituents to inform them (as opposed to the one-to-one situation of the surgery, which the constituent only attends when s/he has a specific problem;

- regular Parliamentary report detailing performance of all MSPs in areas including attendance, voting records, speeches made and so on.

11.2 There was some obvious concern about the delineation of duties between regional and constituency MSPs: for example, the Scottish Council for Development and Industry stated that the electorate was in need of guidance on the roles and responsibilities of each type of MSP, and Clackmannanshire Council suggested that, in the case of list MSPs, the party rather than the individual was made accountable to the electorate.

11.3 Other respondents suggested that meaningful feedback to the electorate could only be achieved if MSPs were given job descriptions, set measurable targets and their performance monitored as happens in any other modern workplace. Not only business organisations took the view that the Parliamentary mystique should be removed and a more businesslike environment created: The Scottish Wildlife Trust, UNISON Scotland and the Scottish Higher Education Funding Council were in favour of variations on such an approach.

12. *Should there be a code of conduct of MSPs and if so what should it cover?*

13. *How might equal opportunities be addressed in such a code of conduct?*

13.1 There was overwhelming support for the instigation of a Code of Conduct for MSPs, with a substantial number of respondees citing the reports of the Nolan Committee and the proposed new Ethical Framework for Local Government as good starting points in determining the content of the Code. Local authorities, in particular, were adamant that any Code of Conduct imposed upon MSPs should be at least as rigorous as that now in place for members of local government. Most respondees who went into detail about the suggested content of the Code envisaged that it would cover lobbying and the Register of MSPs' interests, and should be broad enough to include standards on training, attendance and so on, but there was some dissent as to whether the Code should limit itself to the public aspects of MSPs' lives, or whether it should take in also their private and moral standards of behaviour. There was also a lack of agreement on the issue of whether MSPs should be able to hold other, part time employment while a Member of the Scottish Parliament. Some respondees (such as the Glasgow Association of Women Graduates) felt strongly that the job of the MSP should be a full-time one, while others argued that the Scottish political scene could only benefit from the cross fertilisation of ideas which would result from the involvement of business people active in various fields simultaneously.

13.2 In terms of how equal opportunities could be integrated into such a code, there were few specific, practical suggestions made - more generally - a commitment towards equal opportunities within the code was regarded as desirable. Grampian Racial Equality Council, as an example, emphasised the need for practical guidelines to ensure that the theoretical commitment to equal opportunities was translated into a positive reality. UNISON Scotland suggested that the equal opportunities policy enshrined within the Code of Conduct should follow the model of industrial relations practices.

14. ***What arrangements should be made for the regulation of MSPs' interests?***

14.1 Again, arrangements in Westminster with particular reference to the findings of the Nolan Committee were regarded as a good starting point for regulating MSPs' external interests. The Scottish Parent Teacher Association suggested that the Register of Interests could take on a positive, as well as a negative regulatory role for MSPs, in that it could genuinely give details of topics of particular interest to them, thus allowing interested parties to contact hem directly. In general, it was felt that the Register of Interests should be completely open, and should be available to the public to peruse as they wished, either in the Parliament building itself or in public access points such as libraries. It was also hoped that the Register could be available electronically.

15. ***Should there be regulation of the process of lobbying of MSPs?***

15.1 There was a huge spectrum of views on the topic of lobbying, ranging from unrestricted access, through regulation, to outlawing. Largely this stemmed from general difficulties about defining lobbying: those seeking to ban it completely focused on the professional lobbying companies (this view was put forward by the Scottish Green Party), while those looking for unrestricted access were often those from the voluntary sector which considered lobbying as a legitimate means of accessing the Parliament and its MSPs. Overall, most organisations were looking to see some form of regulation, but in as loose a form as possible so that the balance always lay in favour of organisations wishing to gain access to the Parliament. While in general it was considered sufficient to control lobbying via the Code of Conduct, there were suggestions, as that from The Institute of Management, that the regulation of lobbying should be controlled as part of the MSP's employment contract, thus re-iterating the "MSP as business employee" school of thought outlined in paragraph 14.1 above.

15.2 A view also emerged from professional organisations that a register of lobbyists should be set up, with all meetings recorded in this and minutes of the meetings available for public scrutiny.

16. ***Taking the current Westminster arrangements as a starting point, would you like to see the Scottish Ministers accounting to the Parliament in different ways?***

16.1 In this instance, arrangements currently existing at Westminster were regarded as more satisfactory than in other areas of practice. Most respondees felt that the best way for Ministers and Junior Ministers to be accountable to the Parliament would be via Committee hearings and some form of question time, although in the latter they were keen to see the event becoming more spontaneous and genuine and, at the same time, less confrontational than Prime Minister's Question Time at Westminster.

16.2 The Scottish Liberal Democrats brought forward the view that MSPs would only be able to hold Ministers truly accountable if access to civil service briefing was available to all members of the Parliament, and not only to members of the Executive. They considered that such a shift in the remit of civil servants should be made as: "The opportunity to abolish the culture of secrecy and deliberate obfuscation which pervades Whitehall should be taken as soon as possible."

Accessible, Open, Responsive.

17. ***What steps might the Parliament take to develop an accessible culture?***

18. ***How can it make its working practices transparent and understandable?***

19. ***How should it ensure that people have information about the Parliament?***

19.1 Many of the ideas outlined in the other sections of this report are seen to be at the heart of accessibility to the Parliament. For example, it is hoped that if groups and individuals have regular access to their MSPs and are not intimidated by arcane ceremonies, they will feel that the Parliament is closer to them. Similarly, mechanisms for sharing the power, reaching disadvantaged groups, and mainstreaming equal opportunities are all regarded as playing an important role in developing an accessible culture.

19.2 The following ideas were all suggested in responses:

- Libraries as information points (suggested by the Scottish Green Party).

- Public information service.

- Internet (all documents and summaries)and including a "virtual tour".

- Helpdesk.

- Education facilities and material.

- Public information service.

- As well as providing all documents and papers on the Internet, these should be available to purchase at cost price.

- Simple ceremonies.

- Plain English both written and spoken: Scottish Law Commission emphasised need for legislation itself to be comprehensible to the lay person and to follow the example of recent rewrites of tax laws at Westminster.

- Capability Scotland: guidelines on the Parliament to be sent to each household.

20. ***Should there be special arrangements put in place for schools?***

20.1 There was a very strong feeling that there should indeed be special arrangements for schools, and a civic education programme with possible material produced by the Parliament for use by pupils, especially those nearing the voting age, was favoured. In this connection, organisations (such as WEA Scotland) also asked that adult education be considered as a key to ensuring genuine participation from all sectors of Scottish society. This should be backed up by dedicated tours of the Parliament for young people and school groups, and consideration should be given to the establishment of a parallel "Youth Parliament" for young people. Respondents also noted that schools could be used to broaden out access to the Parliament for others, because their established Internet networks could become general information access points for the public.

21. ***What Committee structure should the Parliament create?***

21.1 There were a whole host of ideas emerging from the consultation exercise which attempted to prescribe possible Committee structures which the Parliament might create. Evidently, this manifested itself largely in interest groups advocating particular Committees which related to their constituency - for example, a Committee on Equality (supported by a Minister and an Equality Unit) was supported by the Equality Network and endorsed by other equal opportunities groups and a Children's Committee was suggested by the Royal College of Paediatrics and Child Health and Children in Scotland. Rape Crisis Centre suggested that the example from Glasgow City Council, where the Equality Committee is backed up by various sub Committees should be adopted.

21.2 The issue of the creation of sub-Committees and ad-hoc Committees was also addressed by respondents. For example, Scottish Engineering wished to see permanent Committees complemented by short life Committees to deal with ad-hoc, possibly cross-cutting issues. W J Allan Macartney MEP envisaged a system along the lines of the European Parliament Committee structure, whereby a fixed number of permanent Committees are complemented by a limited number of ad hoc Committees. Other groups such as Alzheimer Scotland wanted to see the use of sub Committees to examine particular policy issues.

21.3 RSPB Scotland and the Scottish Liberal Democrats, among others, also noted that, for a truly powerful Committee structure to be created, Committees would need access to staff and resources (eg a library) independent from Executive control.

21.4 The other significant issue which many of the respondents picked up in terms of the Committee structure was the perceived desirability of having Committees holding evidence taking sessions around Scotland. This idea was extremely popular and was seen as a key to "sharing the power" and overcoming the alienation which was seen to have been caused by a remote Parliament in Westminster.

22. ***Should there be separate select and standing Committees or should there be single Committees investigating the work of government departments and scrutinising legislation?***

22.1 A wide raft of ideas emerged on this issue: some such as the Campaign for a Scottish Parliament, the Green Party and the City of Edinburgh Council felt that there should be single Committees which could develop expertise and which would place less pressure on the MSPs in such a small Parliament. It was also regarded, for example by the Equality Network, as the only way of ensuring an integrated approach to particular issues (such as equal opportunities). Others believed that the scrutiny/legislative functions needed to be separated - for example, a Committee which had been involved in the passing of a particular piece of legislation might not scrutinise its implementation and practical application in the same way as a Committee with no "personal" interest.

23. *Should there be Committees reflecting the structure of the Scottish Office or should they cut across the work of departments?*

23.1 The general feeling emerging from the consultation exercise was that the Committee structure should be cross cutting to allow them to tackle long-term objectives, but there was a recognition that this could cause difficulties in relation to the scrutiny of the Executive, and that such a structure might deliver a constantly changing set of Committees as policy priorities changed over time. Councils and COSLA favoured the "client group" rather than functional approach, mirroring their own model, and believed that such a cross cutting structure would avoid inter-departmental conflicts.

23.2 Another option which enjoyed support was that the Parliament should have a certain number of departmental based Committees backed up by a few strategic Committees which would have an audit role across all departments. SEPA, for example, suggest the need for an equivalent to the House of Commons Environmental Audit Committee which could also scrutinise legislative proposals and check to what extent the policies of departments are in line with principles of sustainability. The Scottish Liberal Democrats proposed that Committees should be predicated on a basic departmental structure, but with an element of holistic government built in by giving each Committee full Executive responsibility for that area, including the impact of other legislation and proposals on it. As in the European Parliament, the lead Committee on a particular piece of legislation would therefore bring in the views of other Committees whose area of work would be impacted upon.

24. *How might equal opportunities be addressed in the work of Committees?*

24.1 This was not an issue which many respondees tackled separately from general questions on both Committee membership and Equal Opportunities issues. The STUC Black Workers Group suggested that automatic Committee membership for all MSPs would ensure the representation of MSPs from minority groups on Committees, while Perth & Kinross Council wanted to see the monitoring of Committees' equal opportunities policies of Committees via performance targets and indicators. BT stressed the significance of inclusive language, while Democratic Left Scotland emphasised that any meaningful equal opportunities policy should place the burden of proof on Committees to demonstrate that they have promoted equality of opportunity.

25. *How should membership of Committees be decided?*

25.1 The theme running through the responses was that representation on Committees should be proportional to the balance of parties within the Parliament, although it was hoped that the Committees, like the Parliament in general, could adopt a consensual working style which was not solely based on adherence to the Party Whip. Respondees also felt that MSPs should be given some choice about which Committees they sat on, thus ensuring that where possible Committees were composed of MSPs with a particular expertise or interest in the subject. Although some equal opportunities groups favoured quotas for minorities or a 50/50 gender balance, most considered that this would not be fair (or practical in such a small Parliament). Rather, they felt that all MSPs should be given the chance to participate equally in Committee work by the provision that all MSPs should sit on a set number of Committees - perhaps two or three. This would ensure representation for female and minority group MSPs. Some groups also suggested that a geographical spread of constituencies should be represented on all Committees, thus ensuring that central belt interests did not dominate.

25.2 A suggestion was also made (for example, by the Scottish Out of School Care Network) that the membership of Committees be reviewed every three years to ensure the continued input of fresh ideas.

26. *How should Committees initiate legislation?*

26.1 There was definite support for the idea that the powers of Committees should be extended in comparison with those at Westminster to include the power to initiate legislation. Indeed, the local government lobby wished to see this extended to give rights to local government to promote (not only private) legislation (for example, this was brought up by the Society of Local Authority Lawyers and Administrators in Scotland.) The use of the powerful Committee structure which relied heavily on public consultation was regarded as providing an opportunity for legislative proposals to be proactive rather than reactive. The City of Edinburgh Council made the suggestion that the timetable of the Parliament should set aside time for the Committees to initiate legislation, and similarly the Scottish Liberal Democrats proposed that Committee proposals should be submitted to the Business Committee for time to be allocated for the Committee's proposal. That Committee would than take the lead in steering the legislation through the pre-legislative, drafting, and full legislative processes.

27. *What role might non-MSPs play in Committees?*

27.1 Two main strands of thought emerged in answer to this question: that non-MSPs should take an active role in Committees themselves, or that their role should be limited to one feeding into Committees via other types of panels and fora.

27.2 Amongst those who envisaged role for non MSP experts and lay people within the Parliamentary Committees themselves, there was by and large a recognition that it would not be feasible, nor democratically accountable, for such individuals to have voting rights within the Committee. What was suggested was that they should input into the Committee through their advisory role and, in the case of specialists, through a dissemination of relevant background knowledge and an examination of witnesses. (Such a view came, for example, from CBI Scotland). And respondees did tackle the issue of how a measure of accountability could be retained in terms of choice of non-MSP Committee members: for example, the Scottish Civic Assembly wanted to see non voting members appointed via an Appointments Committee, while an alternative suggestion on appointment was raised by the Scottish Chambers of Commerce who suggested that non members be appointed to Committees according to the Nolan guidelines for appointments to NDPBs. To ensure the adequate flow of information, Comann nam Parant Locharrain suggested that non-MSP specialists be appointed on a time limited, topic-related basis, thus maximising the relevance of the input from these experts.

27.3 As mentioned in 30.1 above, the alternative structure suggested in a variety of forms was based around the concept that it would be more appropriate for non MSPs to impact upon the work of Parliamentary Committees via a separate structure which in turn flowed into and advised the Committees themselves. These groups were variously envisaged as advisory forums, informal working groups, expert panels, and sub-Committees.

27.4 For example, the SCVO considered that, with Committees being the focus of the work of the Parliament, early or unrefined ideas could be developed via Parliamentary forums, recognised by the Parliament, where the public and interest groups could develop ideas. These groups should be given official recognition and access to all Committees, and should be given Secretariat funding by the Parliament. *"Recognition by the Parliament will represent a commitment by it to ensure the forum is notified of and consulted on all relevant debates and proposals: that it is "in the loop"."*

27.5 Along similar lines, the STUC Black Workers Group proposed advisory forums drawing on the best practice of the recently established Consultative Women's Forum in the Scottish Office, while the SCDI saw a role for advisory panels including MSPs and representatives of civic society. Invited panel members would be unpaid and the panels set up on an ad-hoc basis. They would be chaired by a member of the relevant Committee into which the Panel feeds, thus guaranteeing continuity between the work of the Committee and that of its advisory panel. Along similar lines, ENABLE suggested that civil servants should draw up informal working groups to consider early ideas before they were fully considered by Committees.

28. *How might pre-legislative scrutiny be undertaken?*

28.1 Pre-legislative scrutiny was regarded as a vital mechanism, particularly in the absence of second chamber, and the idea was put forward that MSPs should be able to halt the progress of a Bill if it became apparent that insufficient pre-legislative consultation had taken place. Local authorities in particular were keen to see pre-legislative scrutiny in partnership with local government and the networks to which they have access, and they also favoured public pre-legislative hearings.

28.2 Again, many respondents here saw a role for national representative forums, composed of MSPs and social partners such as representatives from non-governmental organisations, along the lines of the Law Commission, to consider proposals (this was a suggestion, for example from the Children's Panel Chairmen's Group and RSPB). Another example along the same lines emanated from WWF Scotland and the Scottish Local Government Information Unit, who both suggested that a holistic approach to pre-legislative scrutiny be adopted via the formation of a Social Partners Forum, where partners on a specific issue would come together and draw together proposals to be taken forward within the Parliament as legislation.

28.3 The role of Committees in co-ordinating and taking responsibility for the pre-legislative scrutiny process was recognised, for example, by the Scottish Police Federation who supported the establishment of a dedicated Committee for pre-legislative scrutiny.

28.4 Others returned here to the "forums" idea which shaped much of the thinking on the involvement of non MSPs on Committees: for example, the Children's Panel Advisory Committee wished to see wide representation from interested parties in the pre-legislative process via a Consultative Forum; an alternative was proposed by the Scottish Down's Syndrome Association who felt that pre-legislative consultation should take place using the Scottish Civic Assembly as umbrella body. The Scottish Liberal Democrats favoured a consultation process co-ordinated by the ACC (see paragraph 32 below) which would look at the basic legislative proposal and build up a consensus view to be passed back to the Parliament.

28.5 Paragraphs 9.1 and 9.2 above are also relevant here: the consultation process was regarded as inextricable from the pre-legislative process.

29. *How might the views of interest groups and the impact of new policies on them be taken into account before and during the legislative process?*

29.1 This question very much brought together the same kind of responses as questions on Sharing the Power (in particular taking into account the views of civic society) and those on pre-legislative scrutiny and the involvement of non MSPs in the work of Committees. A definite view emerged that the consultation process should begin much earlier to allow interested groups a role in setting the scope and agenda of legislation, rather than commenting on what has already been produced. The Law Society of Scotland and others came out in favour of a continuation of the Green Paper/White Paper approach, which was regarded as working reasonably well and which had the advantage of being familiar to consultees.

29.2 The Poverty Alliance made the suggestion that there should be an accreditation process for voluntary groups, in particular umbrella organisations, who would themselves act as networks to bring together views on consultation and could then represent views gleaned through their roles as non-voting members of the relevant Committee.

29.3 Other organisations also proposed radical new ways of consulting. For example, RoSPA favoured proactive communication between interested parties with Committees, so that possibilities for submitting evidence to Committees would not be dependent upon receipt of an invitation from that Committee to give evidence: rather, organisations should be able to apply to the Committee asking for their evidence to be heard. Wider consultation should be encouraged: the Scottish Civic Assembly wished to see early consultation being encouraged via the publication of an "issues" paper inviting public response, while the Committee of Scottish Clearing Bankers considered that the first stage in consultation might be an informal process whereby views can be heard in open forums. Several organisations, including Children in Scotland, were keen to see that feedback was given to views brought forward during the consultation process, thus demonstrating that views have been considered.

29.4 The Scottish Liberal Democrats advocated here a Social Partnership model, which would cover consultation at all stages of the legislative process and which would be an organisation to feed in views of non MSPs to Committees. They envisaged the formation of an independent body called the Advisory and Consultative Council (ACC) to which civic organisations would appoint representatives. The ACC would form itself into Committees and would have Parliamentary funding and base itself within the old Royal High School. In this way, the ACC would become a forum for consultation and could also provide expert advice to the Parliament and Executive.

30. *What information should the Parliament take into account when considering proposals (eg financial implications, equal opportunities implications, environmental impact, implications for business)?*

30.1 Here again, groups advocated the consideration of implications which were connected to their area of interest. A compliance cost assessment and consideration of long term economic effects was supported CBI Scotland *"Legislative proposals should always include a section dealing with the costs and/or economic benefits of what is proposed both in direct terms and the indirect effect on the economy as a whole",* and the Scotch Whisky Association. The Scottish Liberal Democrats also focused on the particular significance of financial implications: they considered it necessary to avoid narrow "Treasury style" control. Instead, proposals should be presented to the Parliament with full financial information, including costings for alternatives, and civil servants should provide non Executive parties with costings of proposals as necessary.

30.2 Councils were keen to see potential legislation proofed in regard to its potential impact on local government (in particular, the resources local authorities would need to implement the legislation and whether it would erode local government functions) Other examples of the kinds of implications to be considered were:

• Health Education Board for Scotland - health implications;

• Engender: gender implications.

• North Ayrshire Council - implications for rural areas;

• Save the Children Fund - adherence to the UN Convention of the Rights of the Child;

• Equal Opportunities Commission - equal opportunities implications, monitored by an Equality Unit.

31. *How can the Parliament ensure that legislation is properly considered?*

31.1 The response to this which was widely given was that the timetable of the Parliament must be published well in advance to allow any groups with interests to consult widely and prepare their response. Such consultation should also avoid badly conceived legislation as end users will have chance to make their views known. This could be monitored by an independent structure which would audit the quality and quantity of consultation (as per the PHACE West response) Similarly, the use of a structured timetable would avoid the use of measures such as the guillotine which cut off debate (British Federation of Women Graduates). Limited debate at each stage would ensure all clauses of a Bill have the chance to be equally considered. The Institute of Chartered Accountants of Scotland wanted to see a "breathing space" built into the course of legislation to allow for further reflection and consultation. A similar view that the consultation process should not stop with the introduction of a Bill was advocated by The Royal Society of Edinburgh: *"During the passage of a Bill, the appropriate Committee should continue to receive representations and adequate time must be allowed for the amended Bill to be considered. Defects in Bills are often due to amendments having been made without adequate opportunity to reconsider the Bill in its entirety."*

31.2 Similarly the "quality not quantity" principle to the introduction of legislation was favoured, for example by COSLA. Following the same idea as that which had been advocated by the Scottish Liberal Democrats in terms of MSPs' appreciation of the financial implications of proposed legislation, the Committee of Scottish Clearing Bankers considered that ill formed legislation could be avoided if civil servants provided briefing to all MSPs, not just the Executive, so that they are fully informed.

32. *Should existing legislation be reviewed and if so, how? What factors might be taken into account (eg financial implications, equal opportunities implications, environmental impact, implications for business)?*

32.1 There was some concern about the resource implications of any widespread programme to review all legislation, and the "if it's not broken, don't mend it" view was voiced by many organisations. Two other views became apparent: that new legislation introduced within the Scottish Parliament should be reviewed as part of a post-legislative scrutiny process, and that existing Westminster legislation should be reviewed and "Scottified". For example, the Scottish Association for the Study of Delinquency saw a role for Committees in reviewing legislation 3/5 years after its implementation against milestones agreed at that time. The Federation of Small Businesses suggested that all new legislation should be reviewed one year after its implementation, by a different Committee to that responsible for its legislative passage. The need for the "Scottification" of legislation was supported by The Scottish Liberal Democrats who noted that much legislation pertaining to Scotland is tacked on at the end of English Acts, and considered that this should be remedied.

32.2 Respondents considered that the same factors should be considered for the review of existing legislation as for proposals for new legislation.

33. *Should there be electronic voting?*

33.1 This question appeared to cause considerable confusion amongst respondees, many of whom took it to refer to electronic voting by the electorate for elections to the Scottish Parliament. Those who recognised that the question referred to the voting procedures in the Plenary sessions of Parliament were very supportive, seeing it as time saving and cost effective, although there was recognition that there would need to be security safeguards and a manual backup. The RNIB also pointed out that any system in place would need to be suitable for use by blind or partially sighted MSPs.

33.2 There was dissent also about whether MSPs should be able to vote from outwith the Parliamentary Chamber. Some believed that this would erode the accountability of MSPs, and could lead to badly conceived legislation as MSPs could vote without being aware of the issues raised in debate. Others considered that a remote voting system would have the advantage of allowing MSPs in remote areas to participate in the proceedings without the need to travel to Edinburgh.

34. *How can it make the best use of Information Technology, the Internet, electronic mail?*

34.1 Issues of Information and Communication Technology related also to the discussion on Sharing the Power (access to information about the work of the Parliament); Equal Opportunities (how to ensure all individuals and groups had similar access to information) and Accountability (how members of the public could contact and be aware of the work of their MSPs). Thus ICT was regarded as being useful as a conduit for two way communication - both for the dissemination of information and for the facilitation of consultation and the garnering of public opinion. It was widely felt, for example, that all MSPs and Committees should be accessible by e-mail, and that discussion groups should be set up on the Internet.

34.2 For the Parliament to become a showpiece for best use of ICT, there should be broad and imaginative use of information technology, for example, taking Committee evidence by video-conferencing with remote areas, or as the Glasgow's Children's Panel Advisory Committee suggested, by using an interactive website.

34.3 The need to recognise that sophisticated ICT systems were not available to all was emphasised in this part of the discussion (as throughout the responses) and CD-ROM, for example, was considered an inexpensive alternative to the provision of Parliamentary information via the Internet for those without on-line access. Similarly, ICT Best Practice should include the provision of ICT access points (as suggested by British Telecom) in councils, supermarkets, schools, libraries and so on.

35. *What other Best Practice could the Parliament draw on?*

35.1 Respondents considered that the best source of best practice would be other Parliaments, particularly those which were devolved and/or related to areas with similar populations to Scotland. BT cited the example of the Swedish Parliament, where the website showed the contents of the Prime Minister's mailbag each day. The United Nations and the European Union were also mentioned as worth considering in their use of social partners and a participative approach to decision making. Local Government examples were suggested by councils themselves, and by Strathclyde Fire Board who suggested that the Parliament should adopt Local

Government's "best value" approach, both in its planning cycle and in terms of procedures and systems which should be benchmarked against those in other countries. The Irish National Economic and Social Forum was also cited several times as an example of best practice in consultation.

35.2 Turning around the question, John G Sturrock expressed the hope that the innovative new working methods of the Parliament should result in a new model of best practice for the rest of Scotland through its consensus building politics.

Equal Opportunities

36. ***The Scottish Parliament is likely to keep normal business hours and take Scottish school holidays. What else should it take into account to ensure that the Parliament is open to all?***

36.1 The issue of the Parliament keeping normal business hours and taking Scottish school holidays was broadly supported, but not universally. It did attract some criticism as it was felt that such a timetable might work against the principle of accessibility, as it might exclude those who work or attend school themselves from being able to visit the Parliament while it is in session. Some business organisations, such as FirstGroup plc, also felt that it would be non-businesslike for the Parliament to place such restrictions on its working hours. The proposal was made (for example by the National Board of Nursing), therefore, that some consideration should be given to allowing out of hours public access to the Parliament, ensuring that everyone had the opportunity to visit.

36.2 Women's and children's organisations were also very supportive of the provision of nursery facilities but, it was felt that these should be available not only for MSPs, but for staff and visitors. In a similar vein, it was regarded as important to remember that access to meetings could be restricted for example by their timing (during religious holidays or at times when organising childcare might be difficult) or by access difficulties (such as the availability of signers or interpreters, or whether pre-meeting material was available in good time in Braille format). Access to public transport was identified, for example by Business & Professional Women UK Ltd and the West Lothian Women's Forum as another key to providing the opportunity for all to participate in the Parliament.

37. ***What other practices could be adopted to promote equal opportunities?***

37.1 Equal opportunities organisations in particular advocated a wide variety of measures which would both ensure equality of opportunity within the Parliament and which would also send a signal to the rest of Scotland indicating the Parliament's position as a model of equal opportunities best practice. For example, the Equal Opportunities Commission suggested that all Parliamentary funded bodies should provide Equal Opportunities plans including performance objectives and monitoring mechanisms as a condition of their funding. ENABLE asked that the Parliament embrace the principle of "reasonable adjustment", by which any policy, procedure or practice might have to be changed to allow the participation of a particular group.

37.2 Many organisations, such as Capability Scotland also suggested that a welcoming atmosphere on arrival in the Parliament could be created if disability (and other equal opportunities) training were to be provided for staff. There was also a recognition that any equal opportunities policy in the Parliament could only be meaningful if it were monitored regularly and relevant statistics collected: COSLA suggested that such monitoring could be undertaken by a Parliamentary Unit along the lines suggested in the John Wheatley Centre report.

37.3   Fife Council Service Development Team made a particular point about the need to ensure that methods of consultation in themselves encouraged equality of opportunity: *"The Parliament should be proactive in seeking minority women's views and translating them into the legislative process rather than drafting legislation and then assessing the impact upon disadvantaged groups"*. They felt that only in this way could the Parliament ensure that the consultation process spreads beyond the powerful groups with the resources to make their voices heard.

38.   *How might the language and other practices of the Parliament be inclusive/non-discriminatory?*

38.1   It was generally recognised that English would be the main language of the Parliament, but various organisations lobbied for the use in the proceedings of other languages. Such views were not restricted to discussion of Gaelic and but also related to ethnic minority languages and the status of BSL, which, for example, the Royal National Institute of the Deaf said should be recognised as an official language of the Scottish Parliament. It was widely considered that translation of documents into Braille, Gaelic, ethnic minorities languages and non-traditional formats (such as tapes) were a key to ensuring accessibility to information, as was the use of non-sexist language (eg make alternate use of male and female forms in all written documents)

38.2   Organisations such as Comunn na Gaidhlig and sister organisations asked that Gaelic should be given particular status in the Parliament: It was also recommended that *"constituents should be granted a right to use Gaelic in their dealings with Parliament and to expect the use of Gaelic in reply"*. They also argued that MSPs should have the right to use Gaelic in all Parliamentary proceedings, making its status on a par with that of English.

38.3   Several groups (particularly those in peripheral areas of Scotland) also highlighted the need to consider regional issues in the context of ensuring the inclusivity of the Parliament. For example, the Scottish Liberal Democrats and the Shetland Islands Council Liberal Democrat Group both emphasised the need to see adequate representation for the regions and island areas, and they proposed particular Committees to cover the particular needs of these areas, backed up by an "Islands Desk" within the civil service. Similarly, the Scottish Conservatives in the Dumfries area proposed that inclusivity could be promoted by distributing Government departments around Scotland to areas relevant to each department.

ANALYSIS OF RESPONSES TO THE CSG CONSULTATION EXERCISE RECEIVED BY 31 JULY 1998

TOTAL = 336

including:-

By E- mail = 6

Submissions to CSG treated as responses = 21

Confidential = 6

Breakdown

Business Organisations = 53

Education Bodies = 36

Health Bodies = 32

Individuals = 36

Local Government = 31

Museums and Arts = 6

Other = 22

Political Parties = 7

Professional Organisations = 32

Public Services = 3

Religious Organisations = 12

Voluntary Sector = 52

Women's Groups =14

LIST OF (NON-CONFIDENTIAL) RESPONDEES TO THE CSG CONSULTATION EXERCISE

Professional Bodies

- Association of Chartered Certified Accountants
- Association of Chief Police Officers in Scotland
- Association of Consulting Engineers
- Association of Principal Fire Officers
- Association of Professional Foresters
- Association of Scottish Police Superintendents
- BMA
- Brewers and Licensed Retailers Association of Scotland
- British Dental Association
- Broadcasting Council for Scotland
- Chartered Institute of Building
- Chartered Institute of Public Finance & Accountancy
- Committee of Scottish Clearing Bankers
- Construction Industry Training Board
- Council for Professions Supplementary to Medicine
- East of Scotland Association Institution of Civil Engineers
- Fire Officers' Association
- Institute of Chartered Accountants of Scotland
- Institute of Directors
- Institute of Management
- Law Society for Scotland
- Malt Distillers Association of Scotland
- National Association of Estate Agents

- Offshore Operators Association Ltd
- Royal Incorporation of Architects in Scotland
- Royal Institution of Chartered Surveyors in Scotland
- Royal Town Planning Institute in Scotland
- Scotch Whisky Association
- Scottish & Northern Ireland Plumbing Employers' Fed
- Scottish Assessors' Association
- Scottish Association of Chief Building Control Officers
- Scottish Association of Meat Wholesalers
- Scottish Decorators Federation
- Scottish Engineering
- Scottish Grocers Association
- Scottish Law Commission
- Scottish Pig Industry Initiative
- Scottish Police Federation
- Scottish Tourism Forum
- Sheriff's Association
- Society of Chief Officers of Trading Standards in Scotland
- Society of Local Authority Lawyers & Administrators
- Society of Directors of Personnel
- Virus Tested Stem Cuttings Growers' Association

HEALTH BODIES

Boards

- Argyll & Clyde Health Board
- Ayrshire & Arran Health Board
- Fife Health Board
- Forth Valley Health Board
- Greater Glasgow Health Board

- Health Education Board for Scotland

- Lanarkshire Health Board

- National Board for Nursing, Midwifery....

- Tayside Health Board

Trusts

- Ayrshire & Arran Community Healthcare NHS Trust

- Falkirk & District Royal Infirmary NHS Trust

- Hairmyres & Stonehouse Hospitals NHS Trust

- Lanarkshire Healthcare NHS Trust

- North Ayrshire & Arran NHS Trust

- Perth & Kinross Healthcare NHS Trust

- Raigmore Hospital NHS Trust

- Royal Infirmary of Edinburgh NHS Trust

- South Ayrshire Hospitals NHS Trust

- Waverley Care

- Yorkhill NHS Trust

Hospitals

- Queen Margaret Hospital

- Royal College of Paediatrics and Child Health

Associations

- Scottish Association for Mental Health

- Scottish Association of Health Councils

- Scottish Down's Syndrome Association

Other

- Action on Smoking and Health (Scotland)

- Centre for Scottish Public Policy Health Commission

- Dumfries & Galloway Health Council

- General Dental Council

- Greater Glasgow Health Council

- Institute of Health Services Management

- Mental Welfare Commission for Scotland

- Royal College of Surgeons of Edinburgh

- UK Central Council for Nursing

LOCAL GOVERNMENT

- Aberdeen City Council

- Aberdeenshire Council

- Angus Council

- Association of Scottish Community Councils

- City of Edinburgh Council

- Clackmannanshire Council

- Dundee City Council

- Fife Council

- Fife Council - Corporate Policy Service

- Glasgow City Council

- Highland Council

- Inverclyde Council

- Midlothian Council

- Moray Council

- North Ayrshire Council

- North Lanarkshire Council

- Perth & Kinross Council

- Renfrewshire Council

- Scottish Borders Council

- Scottish Local Government Information Unit

- Scottish Local Authorities Economic Development Group

- Shetland Islands Council

- South Lanarkshire Council

- West Dunbartonshire Council

- West Lothian Council

- Convention of Scottish Local Authorities

- COSLA's Rural Affairs Forum

- Society of Local Authority Chief Executive Officers

- SNP Group, North Lanarkshire Council

VOLUNTARY SECTOR

- Aberdeen City Council Children's Panel & Advisory Committee

- Age Concern Scotland

- Alzheimer Scotland - Action on Dementia

- ARP/050

- Barnardos Scotland

- Barony Care Services

- British Association for Shooting and Conservation

- Capability Scotland

- Centre for Education for Racial Equality in Scotland

- Centre for Racial Equality in Scotland

- Childline Scotland

- Children First

- Children in Scotland

- Children's Panel Advisory Group

- Commission for Racial Equality

- **ENABLE**
  - Engender

  - Epilepsy Association of Scotland

  - Equality Network

  - Forth Friend

- Glasgow Children's Panel Advisory Committee

- Grampian Racial Equality Council

- Guide Association

- Moray Voluntary Service Organisation

- National Foster Care Association

- NCH Action for Children Scotland

- One Plus: One Parent Families

- Poverty Alliance

- Rape Crisis Centre

- Reach Out Highland

- Renfrewshire Elderly Forum

- Royal National Institute for Deaf People

- Royal National Institute for the Blind

- Royal Society for the Prevention of Accidents

- RSPB Scotland

- Save the Children Fund

- Scotland for Children Campaign

- Scottish Childminding Association

- Scottish Council for Voluntary Organisations

- Scottish Fisherman's Association

- Scottish Natural Heritage

- Scottish Out of School Care Network

- Scottish Wildlife Trust

- Strathclyde Elderly Forum

- Stresswatch Scotland

- United Kingdom Home Care Association Ltd

- Victim Support Scotland National Office

- Volunteer Development Scotland

- Waverley Care

- WWF Scotland

- YMCA Scotland

- Youthlink Scotland

WOMEN'S GROUPS

- British Federation of Women Graduates

- Engender

- Glasgow Association of Women Graduates

- National Council of Women of Great Britain

- Rape Crisis Centre

- Soroptimist International of Aberdeen

- Soroptimist International of Crieff

- Soroptimist International of Dundee

- Soroptimist International of Glasgow South

- Soroptimist International of Hamilton

- Soroptimist International of Scotland South

- Soroptimist International of West Lothian

- West Lothian Woman's Forum

- Woman's National Commission

- Women onto Work

BUSINESS

- Atlantic Telecom Group

- Automobile Association

- BBC

- BP Scotland

- British Energy plc

- British Retail Consortium

- BT Scotland

- Business and Professional Women UK Ltd

- Business Enterprise Scotland

- Caledonian Brewing Company Ltd

- CBI

- Chartered Institute of Transport in the UK

- Confederation of British Industry, Scotland

- Dumfries & Galloway Enterprise

- Federation of small Businesses

- FirstGroup plc

- Forestry Contracting Association Ltd

- Forum of Private Business

- Glasgow Chamber of Commerce

- Glasgow Development Agency

- Highlands & Islands Enterprise

- Institute of Trading Standards Administration

- Landscape Institute

- Meat and Livestock Commission

- Media Factory

- Scottish Chambers of Commerce

- Scottish Construction Clients Forum

- Scottish Council Development & Industry

- Scottish Enterprise

- Scottish Federation of Housing Associations

- Scottish Industry Forum

- Scottish Power

- Scottish Seafood Project

- Scottish Quality Trout

- Seafood Scotland

SELECT

- Society for Computers and Law

- Specialist Cheesemakers Association

- Stationery Office (Scotland)

- Strathclyde Passenger Transport

- Sun Microsystems Scotland

- Thornburn Colquhoun Consulting Engineers

- TRANSform Scotland

- UK Offshore Operators Association

EDUCATION BODIES

- Adult Learning Project

- APEX Scotland

- Association of Scottish Colleges

- Association of University Teachers (Scotland)

- Catholic Education Commission - Scotland

- Centre of Public Policy & Management

- Comann nam Parant Locharrain

- Committee of Vice-Chancellors & Principals

- Community Education Managers Scotland

- Comunn na Gaidhlig

- Education for Sustainable Development Group

- Educational Broadcasting Council for Scotland

- Educational Institute of Scotland

- Equal Opportunities Commission

- General Teaching Council for Scotland

- Institute of Personnel & Development

- Meat Training Council

- Museum Training Institute

- National Library for Scotland

- National Union of Students Scotland

- PHACE West

- Student's Representation Council, Glasgow University

- University of Dundee

- Professional Association of Teachers Scotland

- Professor Ronan Paddison & Dr Barbara Jeffrey

- Royal Society of Edinburgh

- Scottish Consultative Council on the Curriculum

- Scottish Council of National Training Organisations

- Scottish Further Education Unit

- Scottish Higher Education Funding Council

- Scottish Interactive Technology Centre

- Scottish Library & Information Council

- Scottish Library Association

- Scottish Parent Teacher Council

- Scottish Training Federation

- Scottish Qualifications Authority

- Scottish School Sports

- Secretary of State's Advisory Group on Education for Sustainable Development

- Worker's Education Association

MUSEUMS AND ARTS

- Comunn na Gaidhlig

- SALVO

- Scottish Arts Council

- Scottish Arts Network

- Scottish Museums Council

- Scottish Museums Federation

PUBLIC SERVICE

- North Joint Police Board

- Strathclyde Fire Board

- Strathclyde Fire Brigade

RELIGIOUS

- Action of Churches Together in Scotland (Acts)

- Baptist Union of Scotland

- Christian Education Movement in Scotland

- Church of Scotland

- Church of Scotland Guild

- Council for Scottish Jewry

- Evangelical Alliance

- Holy Trinity Metropolitan Community Church

- Scottish Inter Faith Consultative Group

- Society, Religion & Technology Project

INDIVIDUALS

- Adrienne R Murray

- Aileen Welsh

- Archibald Macpherson

- Barbara Simon

- Bernard Crick

- Bob McCubbin

- Christina H Buchanan

- Councillor Gordon Murray JP

- Craig Cockburn

- David M Elliot
- Dr Diarmid J G Weir
- Dr Eilidh M Whiteford
- Dr W J Allan McCartney MEP
- Duncan M Butlin
- Earl of Mar & Kellie
- E M Forbes
- Edith Clark
- Eurig Scandett
- George Walker
- Gillian D Grant
- Ian M G Smith
- Irene Hamilton
- Isobel E Fraser
- James Graham
- Jean Hunter
- Jim Cuthbert
- John G Sturrock
- John N Moor
- KC Fraser
- Keith Burstein
- K MacArthur
- Mark Dennis
- M Shields
- Malcolm A Ritchie
- Mark Chadwick
- Norman Tinlin
- Peter Carr

- Rev John McLean

- Rev P Moore

- Ronald Johnson

- Russell Taylor

- S Duff

- Sir George Elliot

- Sir Iain Noble

- S Mitchell

- Susan Moffat

- Thomas MacPherson

- Wlliam McCallum

- W J Allan Macartney (MEP)

OTHER

- British Motorcyclists Federation

- Campaign for a Scottish Parliament

- Charter 88 Glasgow

- Charter 88 Scotland

- Children's Panel (Aberdeen)

- Children's Panel Advisory Committee (Edinburgh)

- Children's Panel Chairmen's Group

- Comataidh Craolaidh Gaidlig (Gaelic Broadcasting Committee)

- Democratic Left Scotland

- Dumfries & Galloway Tourist Board

- East of Scotland Water

- Edinburgh & Lothians Tourist Board

- Edinburgh Bisexual Group

- Edinburgh University Bisexual, Lesbian or Gay Society

- Fair Play Scotland

- Glasgow University LGB Society

- Institution of Economic Development, Scotland

- Moredun Research Institute

- Motorcycle Action Group (Scotland)

- National Trust for Scotland

- North of Scotland Electricity Consumers' Committee

- Perthshire Tourist Board

- Pubic and Commercial Services Union

- Royal Society of Edinburgh

- Scottish Association for the Study of Delinquency

- Scottish Campaign for Nuclear Disarmament

- Scottish Children's Reporter Administration

- Scottish Civic Assembly

- Scottish Environment Protection Agency

- Scottish Green Party

- Scottish Liberal Democrats

- Scottish Sports Council

- SEPA - Scottish Emergency Planning

- Shetland Islands Council Liberal Democrat Group

- STUC - Black Workers Committee

- UNISON Scotland

ANNEX E

NOTE OF THE MAIN POINTS ARISING AT THE CONSULTATIVE STEERING GROUP (CSG) OPEN FORUM MEETINGS: JULY TO AUGUST 1998

Galashiels

Pre-Legislative Scrutiny

- In the absence of a second chamber in the Scottish Parliament, important for all legislation to be properly scrutinised.

- Consideration should be given to an "implementation phase" to allow local government and businesses the opportunity and the time required to prepare for implementation of legislation.

Participation

- Important for Scottish Parliament Committees to take into consideration the views of the people.

- Participation should also be encouraged at local government level so that regions, areas and communities are geared up to input to central policy development.

- Individuals, groups and organisations must be prepared for a new form of participative Government.

Sharing the Power

- Important for decisions not to be made remotely; local people must have a say.

- Views of local people in areas such as Newcastleton should be taken into account. Villagers should feel a part of "sharing the power".

- Open Forum meetings and Focus Group sessions were a useful step towards enfranchising people in rural communities.

- ICT could be a useful mechanism to open up debate although implementation costs could be high. However, more traditional methods of communication would still be required.

- MSPs should be obliged to consult community councils.

- Local authorities too large to allow proper contact with people living in rural communities.

- Advent of the Scottish Parliament as another layer of Government would make matters even more confusing.

- Public should feel that the Parliament is more accessible and more receptive to their views.

- Local decisions could be taken at a more local level rather than at a central level.

Quangos

- Quangos need to be made more accountable.

- The appointment of people to quangos should be more transparent, democratic and accountable.

Culture of the Parliament

- Scottish Parliament should make maximum use of ICT both externally and internally and should also use electronic voting in elections.

- Seating arrangements should be less confrontational.

Working Hours

- Parliament should adopt normal business hours and should also observe Scottish school holidays.

Industry

- Industry could be faced with conflicting legislation from the Scottish Parliament, Westminster and the European Union.

Committees

- First Minister should chair a Health Sub-Committee whose aim would be to consider public health issues and to develop long term strategies for public health.

Accountability

- Significant lack of trust in local government by the public which the Parliament must address.

- Trust and accountability need to be regained at local level under a Scottish Parliament.

Young People

- The interest of young people in the Scottish Parliament should be stimulated through the use of public meetings and providing information in schools and local areas.

- Information should be available in simple language and MSPs should actively encourage the views of young people.

- Young people should be taught about the democratic process as part of the school curriculum.

Glasgow

Role of the Elderly in the Parliament

- Elderly people should have a greater role in the Scottish Parliament.

- Upper age of Parliament falls short of pensionable age and it is important that needs of senior citizens are addressed, particularly as they comprise 20% of the electoral role.

- Participation among elderly citizens should be encouraged.

Equal Opportunities

- Scottish Parliament should have a Minister for equal opportunities.

Accessibility

- Parliamentary Committees should be accessible and deal with issues cutting across Departmental boundaries.

Consultation

- Equal Opportunity Committee in Glasgow very successful with many significant achievements.

- Essential for Councillors and community organisations including representatives from disabled, elderly, gay groups etc to work together in sub- Committees. This would promote a better structure of consultation.

- Minority groups should be given greater consideration by the Scottish Parliament. Only financially well off groups could hire lobbyists.

- Important to look beyond the list of accredited organisations in consultation process. A Scottish Civic Assembly might be the best way forward as a mechanism to consider particular issues. There must be adequate funding put in place to support a Scottish Civic Assembly.

Electoral Issues

- The age for voting should be lowered to 16 to bring more people into the electoral system.

- There should be changes to the deposit system which currently poses a bar on minority parties.

Accountability of MSPs

- MSPs should be obliged to hold a public audience at least once a year to account for their activities.

Working Hours

- An MSP's job should be full time, working 9am to 5pm Monday to Friday.

Legislation

- Memoranda accompanying Bills should cover employment consequences, implications for staff and for the Scottish economy.

- Proper scrutiny mechanisms would be needed in the absence of a second chamber.

Gaelic

- Hansard and the internet (containing official documents) of the Scottish Parliament should be available in Gaelic. Members of the public should also be able to write to their MSPs in Gaelic and receive a response in Gaelic.

Youth Involvement /Young People's Forum

- All under 25s should be encouraged to be involved in the work of the Parliament.

- A Youth Forum or something similar to the European Youth Parliament could be replicated in Edinburgh.

- Every school should have a dedicated terminal to access the business of the Scottish Parliament.

- Modern Studies important in the school curriculum.

- Important for school children to become involved in the work of the Parliament.

- Use of technology, particularly the web, e-mail, debates on television etc very important.

- MSPs should be available for questioning by the electorate.

- There should be a Children's Issues Committee. Young people need to be encouraged and greater use should be made of ICT.

Further Devolution

- Devolution should be extended so that people living in deprived areas could have a greater say in managing local affairs.

- This would give councils, tenants etc greater scope to work in partnership.

Parliament Building - Smoke Free

- Scottish Parliament building should be a smoke free zone.

Disabled

- Scottish Parliament should give priority to the Incapable Adults Bill.

Dumfries

Remote Areas

- Important that the Scottish Parliament is not dominated by urban areas.

- There should be structures and mechanisms put in place to input a pre-legislative stage or screening of legislation to involve all rural areas.

- There should be screening to take account of the impact of proposed legislation on rural interests.

Centralisation of Essential Services

- Important that Fire and Police services were not merged in rural areas. Should retain separate identities. Fear of centralisation.

The Role of Young People

- Young people should be encouraged to vote and to become more involved in the Scottish Parliament.

- Important to ensure that young people participate in the Scottish Parliament elections.

- Vital to keep them informed through new forms of technology, dialogue, television and newspapers.

- Scottish Parliament should set up a Civic Forum where youth organisations could meet to discuss legislation and topical issues.

- Young people had stopped joining political parties and they were now joining organisations such as the Wildlife Trust.

- A young person should have been recruited onto the CSG.

- There should be a separate campaign to ensure young people register to vote.

- The SCEC campaign seemed right and relevant.

- Civic education was also important and this should be encouraged at schools.

- There should be a Minister for Young People and/or a Minister for the Voluntary Sector.

Lobbyists

- There should be a distinction made between paid lobbyists and organisations such as the RSPB who also lobby Parliament.

- Lobbying was needed but people were concerned about MSPs taking money to lobby on behalf of organisations.

- There must be proper mechanisms put in place to ensure freedom of speech and also to ensure that policies took into account the needs of rural communities.

- The Cycling Parliamentary Advisory Group had worked well at Westminster and there should be a similar group replicated in Scotland.

- Important for the business sector to be represented in Parliament.

Health

- Scottish Royal Colleges should have direct access to health Committees.

- There should be a quick response team set up to consider health issues quickly and effectively.

Education

- There should be no significant changes to the roles of the Scottish Parliament and local government in education; Central Government should set the policy agenda and local government should enact it.

Multi-Layers

- Local needs, particularly those of rural areas, may not be reflected in Scottish Parliamentary discussions.

- Links should be formalised between councillors and MSPs.

- There could be a possible political conflict between the Scottish Parliament and Westminster.

- The public could be confused with all the layers of Government.

- Important for the public to be educated on what was happening in Scotland and on the role of MPs, MSPs, MEPs, councillors etc.

Aberdeen

Freedom of Speech

- The Scottish Parliament should encourage freedom of speech.

The Legislative Process

- Changes in education should be brought about by Executive action rather than by law: it was important that this should continue.

Opening Ceremony

- The Opening Ceremony of the Parliament should be simple and dignified.

- The Honours of Scotland should be used and also the pre-1707 mace.

Role of COSLA

- There could be conflict if COSLA is of a different political persuasion to that of the Scottish Parliament.

Care Facilities

- The Scottish Parliament should provide childcare facilities for children from birth and not just for 2-5 year olds.

- Carers for the elderly should also be available.

- There should be care for all dependents and not just for children and the elderly.

Information Technology

- Important to ensure that the Parliament's Information Service is professional and well resourced.

- Parliament could be more accessible with the setting up by the ICT Panel of a website which could include all official documents, developing information for schools, issuing official reports and weekly bulletins, some of which could be aimed at different sections of society.

- Important to consider the needs of people in remote areas which also have to be taken into account.

Gender Balance

- Important to maintain a gender balance in the Scottish Parliament with equal opportunities for all.

Accessibility

- There should be a national suggestions book for the Scottish Parliament. The same network as the national lottery could be used.

Children's Issues

- There should be a Minister for Children.

- Children's panels also important.

Voting Arrangements

- At present, many MPs vote at Westminster without listening to the debate. Important in the new Scottish Parliament for MSPs to hear the debate before voting.

Accountability of MSPs

- MSPs should be accountable to the electorate and should have job descriptions and be subject to performance measurement.

- MSPs should have a Code of Conduct.

- MSPs will have a full workload and should not be able to hold down two jobs. They should be required to announce other interests and then let the electorate decide.

- Important for the electorate to be kept informed at all times.

- There should be greater scrutiny of quangos.

Pre-legislative Process

- With regard to the pre-legislative process, local government would be keen to offer their expertise to the Scottish Parliament.

- There could be a possible role for local government to convene Consultative Committees to consider and scrutinise legislation on behalf of the Parliament.

Roles and Remits of MSPs, MPs and Euro MPs

- The public needs educated on the roles, remits and responsibilities of their MSPs, MPs and MEPs.

Committees

- Tripartite Committees should be established in order to bring in interest groups.

- Although only MSPs would be able to vote, interest groups should be allowed input as non-voting Committee members.

- Committees at Westminster dominated by political parties. Committees needed <u>real</u> power.

Secondary Legislation

- Arrangements for pre-legislative scrutiny of primary legislation should also apply to secondary legislation.

- Unlike Westminster, there should be opportunities for the Scottish Parliament to amend secondary legislation.

Inverness

Scottish Fisheries

- Important for Scottish Fisheries to be fully listened to under a new Scottish Parliament.

- Scottish Ministers should be fully involved with other UK Ministers in settling UK issues.

- Scottish Parliament should scrutinise European documents in relation to issues such as fishing.

Committees

- Committees should be able to meet in other areas outwith Edinburgh and, in particular, in remote areas.

- Funded visits to both the Scottish and European Parliaments should be considered.

- It would be wrong to group all rural issues into one Committee.

- There is a need for health, social work and housing to work together. Committee structures should reflect this.

Accessibility of the Parliament

- With regard to petitions it is easier to collect 10,000 signatures in Edinburgh than in a remote area. Important to take population densities into account.

- Scottish Parliament should be as accessible to someone living in Shetland as it is to someone living in the central belt.

- New technology important. Information terminals could be situated all over Scotland to give the public easy access to information.

Powers of the Scottish Parliament

- With the advent of the Scottish Parliament there could be too many layers of Government and Scotland could be in danger of becoming over governed. Important that the Scottish Parliament does not take over the powers of local government.

The Regional Dimension

- Scope for more regional bodies eg Strathclyde Transport.

- Highlands and Islands Convention a good and unique model.

- There should be a Regional Assembly where all MSPs, MPs and MEPs for any one region eg. Highland could come together and discuss common and related issues.

The Parliament

- Normal forms of address should be used in debate and "talking out" should be disallowed.

- Prime Minister's Question Time should not be replicated in the Scottish Parliament.

Access for Disabled

- Alternative formats of publications/documents should be made available including braille and audio tape.

- Important for disabled people to be able to participate in democracy.

- Only 25% of disabled people voted in the last election.

- The electoral process should be more accessible: at present, many polling stations and electoral papers are inaccessible.

- Disabled organisations should be more involved in the pre-legislative process.

Gaelic

- Signage in the Scottish Parliament should be in Gaelic and in other languages.

- Gaelic should play a part in the opening ceremony.

- There should be a Gaelic Committee.

Perth

Trade Union Representation

- There should be Trade Union representation on Scottish Parliamentary Committees and more access for the disabled.

Social Inclusion

- Dealing with social exclusion should have prominence in the Scottish Parliament's agenda.

Scottish Parliament and the Role of Local Government

- There is tension between central government and local government and there is a need to provide strategic direction.

The European Dimension

- Strength of the European Parliament is in having all purpose Committees.

- Question of the revising chamber should be revisited.

- Electronic voting should be considered.

- A joint assembly with MEPs could be established as a consultative mechanism which could meet twice a year, once in Edinburgh and once in Brussels.

Absence of Second Chamber and Role of Interest Groups

- Importance of checks and balances stressed in the absence of a second chamber.

- Essential to use the expertise of interest groups.

Committees

- Departments/Committees should work together, particularly Health and Education.

- Consultation is time consuming and more use could be made of local government quangos and agencies to assist the consultation process.

- Quangos should be brought back under proper democratic control.

- There is a need for a real voice for the poor, unemployed and socially excluded.

- Everyone should understand how the Government operates.

- There is a need for accountability, scrutiny and transparency.

- Important for the Scottish Parliament not to become too central belt orientated. There should be provision for Committee meetings to be held outwith Edinburgh.

Lobbying

- Lobbying should be controlled and there should be a register covering all lobbyists.

Parliamentary Ceremonies

- Scottish Parliamentary ceremonies should be in the Scottish tradition.

Young People

- Important for young people to have access to greater political learning.

- There is widespread confusion about the voting system even among teachers: there should be clarification on the voting system for MSPs.

- Modern Studies important in the school curriculum. Young people needed a fast track system to learn about topical issues.

- Important to educate young people about the Parliamentary process.

Reserved Powers

- Scottish Parliament should have more scope to consider particular issues including energy and broadcasting.

- Consumer Council regulators should be able to work independently. Information should be freely made available.

Racial Issues

- Lack of awareness of race issues in high offices and limited statistics available on ethnic minorities.

- Race issues should be mainstreamed in the Scottish Parliament.

PFI

- The Government should impose a moratorium on PFI projects, for example, the Edinburgh Royal Infirmary, until the Scottish Parliament has been established.

Tensions

- Tensions will arise if different parties are in control in Scotland and at Westminster.

Volunteering Interests

- Important for volunteering interests to be represented in the Scottish Parliament.

Sitting Patterns

- Scottish Parliament should observe business hours and have non-confrontational seating.

Religious Matters

- Scottish Parliament should take into account faiths other than Christian. Use the multi-faith Consultation Council.

Conduct

- There should be no "talking out" of legislation and no publishing of important reports during recess.

User Friendly Legislation

- Legislation should be user friendly.

Research Facilities

- Comprehensive research facilities should be made available to MSPs.

Use of Fora

- Scottish Parliament should think very carefully about the level of consultation on specific issues and whom to consult.

ANNEX F

DRAFT INFORMATION STRATEGY FOR THE SCOTTISH PARLIAMENT

Basic Objective

The Scottish Parliament is committed to providing an Information Service aimed at ensuring that the Parliament is as **open, accessible and participative** as possible. Only well-informed citizens can maximise the opportunities which this presents for individuals and organisations to contribute to the democratic process. Only well informed MSPs can contribute fully to the governance of Scotland. An information strategy, and a well-resourced information service, are vital to the achievement of an ongoing dialogue between Parliament and the People.

Goals for the Parliament's external information services

- to ensure that the public, regardless of gender, age, race, religion or disability, has access to information about the Parliament and its activities;

- to increase the Scottish public's knowledge of, and interest in, Parliament, its work and the democratic avenues which will allow them to contribute to the decision-making process;

- to contribute to the creation of a greater awareness of and respect for the work of the Scottish Parliament and its place in the context of local and national government;

- to provide information in forms which are concise, clear, accurate and attractive.

Goals for the Parliament's internal information services

- to ensure that all MSPs and staff of the Parliament have easy access to the information they need for the effective performance of their duties;

- to give effective support to MSPs and staff of the Parliament in their external information activities concerning the work of the Parliament;

- to respond courteously, promptly and accurately to all requests for information.

Guiding principles

As mentioned above, the Parliament is committed to a style of governance which is welcoming and accessible. In practice, this means that:

- information on the Parliament's functions, work and decisions should be accessible to civic, voluntary and professional organisations, the media, the educational system, local and public authorities, and businesses;

- there must be a Public Information Service dedicated to the provision of such information, whether the enquiry comes by post, telephone, fax, e-mail or in person;

- the information provided by the Public Information Service must be:

  factually correct;

  current;

  non partisan;

  easily available, relevant and understandable, taking into account the needs of the relevant client group;

- the Parliament must take an active role in working with schools, libraries, Citizens' Advice Bureaux, and other organisations, groups and individuals identified by the Parliament in supplying information about the work of the Parliament;

- the Parliament should establish an annual target setting/performance review system for measuring its effectiveness against the background of the general Public Information principles and goals outlined in this Strategy document.

MECHANISMS FOR ENCOURAGING PARTICIPATION: GENERAL

- **Social Partnerships.** Such partnerships may take any form between a loose sense of co-operation between a wider variety of groups in society to a highly specific institutional structure bringing together government, business and labour. Models may be "corporatist" in that a formal relationship is established between government (usually the Executive) and interest groups. Other more fluid, "pluralist" models involve groups operating outside the formal structure of power to influence the decision making process.

- **Consensus Conferences.** Such conferences aim to both inform and consult with citizens by incorporating the perspectives of lay members of civil society within the assessment of new scientific and technological developments. A forum of lay people question experts about a controversial scientific or technological subject, assesses the experts' responses, reaches consensus about the subject and reports its conclusions at a press conference.

- **Citizens' Juries.** These brings together a group of randomly chosen citizens to deliberate on a particular issue (either the setting of a policy agenda or the choice of particular policy options). Over a number of days the jury hears evidence and cross examines witnesses with the help of trained moderators. Following their deliberations, the jury produces a decision or provides recommendations in the form of a citizens' report, obliging some form of response from the department, local authority, or agency.

- **Deliberative Opinion Polling.** Here a national random sample of between 250 and 600 citizens is brought together to discuss and debate a particular issue. Balanced briefing material is provided and citizens can question competing experts and politicians. At the end of the process and after group discussion, citizens are polled in detail.

- **Citizens' Panels.** There are two kinds of citizens' panels: research panels, which use a large sample of a local population as a sounding board to track changes in opinion over time, and standing panels, which are made up of a stable sample of citizens representative of an area's population. The panel meets regularly to assess local services and develop views about future needs and goals, and may be used to test specific policy options or proposals or to scrutinise policy implementation.

- **Public Petitions.** A system of public petitions allows a group of members of the public to indicate their support for a particular cause by gathering signatures which are then presented to the legislature, who may be obliged to take a particular course of action.

MECHANISMS TO FACILITATE PARTICIPATION IN THE WORK OF PARLIAMENTARY COMMITTEES

- **The European Rapporteur system**. A "rapporteur" may be appointed within a Committee for a particular issue on which the Committee is deliberating. The rapporteur has final responsibility for signing the report which the Committee presents to the Plenary, but also acts as a focal point for interest groups and individuals who wish to make representations to the Committee.

- **Expert Panels.** In deliberating on a particular matter, a Committee may wish to set up one or more expert panels where non-members of the Parliament are invited to feed into the Committee's work by advising on areas where they hold expertise. Such a system would be similar to the support provided to CSG by the three Expert Panels.

- **Advisory and Consultative Council (ACC).** This idea is based around the idea of an independent body to which civic organisations would appoint representatives. The ACC would form itself into Committees and would have Parliamentary funding and base itself within the old Royal High School. In this way, the ACC would become a forum for consultation and could also provide expert advice to the Executive and the Parliament and its Committees.

- **Recognition of particular forums** - eg Civic Forum or a Business Forum, which the Executive might be obliged to consult. These could be "official" or "unofficial" as preferred. At the official end of the scale, the bodies might receive some funding from the Parliament.

- **Appointment of specialist advisors.** Select Committees in the UK Parliament already use this mechanism, with both short and long-term appointments.

- **Co-option of non-MSPs.** Committees could co-opt non-voting members, for particular items of business.

MAINSTREAMING EQUALITY IN THE SCOTTISH PARLIAMENT

Introduction

1. The establishment of a Scottish Parliament with law making powers is a unique opportunity to address the issues of equality of opportunity from the outset of a new institution. The aim must be to embed into the process of policy formulation and the way in which the Parliament works, the principles and commitment to promote equal opportunities for all and to eliminate the effects of past discrimination. This paper outlines a set of proposals to the Consultative Steering Group which will enable the Scottish Parliament to ensure that it promotes equal opportunities in the conduct of its business.

2. **The Equal Opportunities Commission** which is sponsored by the Department for Education and Employment is the statutory body charged with upholding the Sex Discrimination Act 1975 and Equal Pay Act 1970 and promoting equal opportunities generally between women and men. It has a Commissioner for Scotland and an office in Scotland with a Director, a Principal Legal Officer, four specialist staff and five support staff. The EOC's Head Office is in Manchester. In 1995 a Scottish Advisory Committee was established to assist with the work in Scotland, and in October 1998 a formal Scotland Committee was established to ensure that the EOC's decision making and work in Scotland are relevant to the new constitutional arrangements.

3. The Equal Opportunities Commission's expertise and statutory remit relates only to discrimination on the grounds of sex and marriage. However, the proposals outlined in this paper are flexible enough to incorporate a broader definition of equality of opportunity.

Mainstreaming equality

4. The EOC wishes to see the promotion of equal opportunities become part of the day to day work of the Scottish Parliament. The notion of "mainstreaming" has developed over recent years as a response to the need to move equal opportunities practices from an "add on" in policy and service development to being an integrated part of an organisation's activities. The advantage of this approach is that it will enable the Scottish Parliament to avoid discriminatory practices, to keep within the law and to ensure that policy and legislation promote equality generally and result in fairer legislation and quality service.

5. More than twenty years after the introduction of the sex and race equality laws, it is clear that much progress has been made in eliminating overt or intentional discrimination. The challenge now is to increase understanding of how inequality arises and is perpetuated, so that the Parliament can ensure that it does not unknowingly discriminate, or by its legislation and practices reinforce past discrimination or inequality.

6. The dictionary defines "inclusive" as "considered together with" or "comprehensive". This fits well with the EOC view of effective "Mainstreaming", which requires:

determination to pursue equality of opportunity and outcome through all policy development, practices, legislation and implementation;

*commitment to scrutinise **before adoption** all legislation and its implementation to identify potential for discrimination.*

commitment in all legislation and its implementation to promote equal opportunities in the relevant areas and to redress inequality and/or differential impact.

an effective mechanism to gather data, evaluate and monitor all services; and a commitment, where there is evidence of inequality and/or differential impact, to assess what changes are required to achieve greater equality and, where possible, to implement these.

Framework for Equality

7. **The legal context:** as an emanation of the British state, the Scottish Parliament will be directly bound by Article 119 of the Treaty of Rome and by the Equal Treatment and Equal Pay directives. These relate to sex equality law. It will also be subject to domestic equality law: The Sex Discrimination Act 1975, Equal Pay Act 1970, Race Relations Act 1976 and Disability Discrimination Act 1996.

8. To give effect to these statutory requirements the Parliament will need to be able to ensure that in its policy making and legislative roles it does not perpetuate past discrimination and that it generally promotes equality. To achieve the conditions for genuine equality, the EOC believes there will also need to be a programme to tackle the historic legacy of inequality.

9. The procedures and structure need to enable the Parliament to avoid and challenge the two types of discrimination defined by law:

- Direct discrimination: treating a person less favourably on the grounds of their sex;

- Indirect discrimination: the imposition of a requirement or condition, applied equally to all, with which a smaller group of one sex cannot comply, so that it causes detriment. This is unlawful if it cannot be objectively justified.

In the next sections the EOC outlines proposals for avoiding discrimination in the conduct of the Parliament's business, for the exercise of its functions with regard to the principle of equality and for using its powers to create equality and inclusiveness across Scotland.

How the Parliament conducts its business

10. Achieving equality, and inclusiveness generally, requires an open style, a willingness to consult and work in partnership with others in the development of plans and policies, backed up by a framework that maintains a momentum, sets standards and timescales and ensures priority for the work in hand.

11. **Defining responsibility:** While the promotion of equal opportunities must be the

responsibility of every MSP and civil servant, it is important to identify clearly where ultimate responsibility for ensuring that the Scottish Parliament meets its obligations lies. This responsibility would normally lie at the most senior level of any organisation. In the case of the Parliament, that would be the Scottish Executive who would delegate to an **Equal Opportunities Committee** on a day to day basis, and to the Permanent Secretary who would similarly delegate to an **Equality Unit.** The EOC was very pleased to note the CSG's support for this proposal.

12.   **An equal opportunities policy statement and plan:**   The Parliament will need to develop and publish a plan detailing the ways in which it intends to fulfil its statutory duty. This should include proposals to eliminate discrimination and promote equality in relation to its role as an employer, the general conduct of its business, how policy and legislation will be appraised for its equality impact, the relationship with external bodies and any services the Parliament provides. It will be important to consult widely, with equality bodies and other agencies with a potential interest, in the drawing-up of this plan. To undertake this task, to provide advice and expertise for the necessary monitoring and scrutiny, and to manage the programme proposed below, there will need to be an **Equality Unit** established within the Scottish Office.

13.   **An Equal Opportunities Committee:**   The Committee's role would be to ensure a focus on equal opportunities issues relating to all the Parliament's activities. It would set priorities, monitor progress and determine action. It would scrutinise policy and legislative proposals and implementation for equality impact. This Committee should establish a structure for close liaison with the statutory and voluntary equality bodies.

14.   **Training:**   It cannot be expected that MSPs and staff will be experts in the fields of equality. A training programme will be an essential part of establishing a framework to promote equality and inclusiveness.

15.   **Collection and disaggregation of data:**   This will be needed to monitor change and chart progress.

Recommendations:

- **That responsibility for ensuring the promotion of equal opportunities and elimination of discrimination through the Parliament's activities should lie with the Scottish Executive**

- **That an Equal Opportunities Committee and an Equality Unit be established for day to day development, monitoring and prioritizing.**

- **That an Equal Opportunities policy statement and plan be agreed and issued by the Parliament as a matter of priority after its establishment.**

- **That a programme of training and the establishment of mechanisms for collection of disaggregated data be established as a priority to prepare the MSPs and staff for the required monitoring and development role.**

The Parliament at Work

16.   **Participation:** The political parties have made their own decisions on arrangements to improve gender equality.   The EOC proposes that, where there is under-representation, provision be made for co-options in an advisory capacity to Committees. Consultation procedures can also be adopted, as routine, to include groups under-represented in membership of the Parliament. Ethnic minority people and disabled people, if elected as MSPs, will require additional support services. Moslems would require prayer facilities. A disabled member may need extra and particular secretarial services, written material produced in large print or other assistance.

17.   **Conditions of work:**   It is clearly important that, in the ways in which it operates, the hours of work, the terms and conditions of staff and MSPs, the Parliament reflects good equal opportunities practice.   The Consultative Steering Group has made recommendations in line with this. The EOC emphasises that the structural and situational barriers to participation in the Parliament can be removed.

- ensuring hours of work are compatible with caring and family responsibilities by working term time and day time hours.
- ensuring that membership of the Parliament is a properly waged activity.
- providing support for child care and other caring needs.
- ensuring that staff and members are able to observe whatever are their own religious holidays and observances.
- additional travel allowances for those with special needs.
- supplementary travel allowances for those with additional needs.

Recommendations:

- **Standing Orders should allow for co-options in an advisory capacity to Committees where there is under-representation of women, ethnic minority people, disabled people or other groups**

- **Standing Orders should provide for a range of support facilities for disabled people as members, visitors or participants in any other capacity**

- **Outreach facilities should be developed with accessible video conferencing (subtitled, audio description, etc.) in publicly accessible venues well used by all sections of the community**

- **Information about the Parliament's role and activities must be available in appropriate minority ethnic languages as well as English and Gaelic, and in Braille, large print and audio description**

- **There must be easy and accessible public transport links to the Parliament**

- **Conditions of work for MSPs must remove social, economic and cultural barriers to participation by previously excluded groups.**

The Decision making Process

18.   **Style of decision making:**   The traditional Westminster style of point-scoring, quick

repartee, aggression and counter-aggression is alienating for most women, people with a different cultural background, many disabled people and indeed, many men. To promote inclusiveness it will be important to set a style that listens to views, seeks to find solutions to problems and allows for the development of constructive argument and debate. This can be achieved through Standing Orders but also by encouraging the establishment of working parties and task groups. Where it is required to reserve matters to a Committee, meetings must be accessible and open in the way in which they operate. A style that encourages consultation with specialists and those with experience in different fields will be important. Parliamentary Committees should involve outside specialists as advisers and establish working parties and consultative fora to assist in achieving consensus and informed decision making.

19.   Also important to creating inclusiveness in decision making is the use of language. As a modern institution, established to take Scotland into the new millennium, it would be appropriate that the Parliament's Standing Orders set the scene for the use of gender-neutral language in written and spoken communication and ensure that language which could offend because of race or disability or sexual orientation is not acceptable in debate.

20.   **Developing a programme approach:**   If the Parliament is to function as a body that promotes and fosters inclusiveness, it needs to consider carefully the ways in which it reaches decisions, determines priorities, ensures that action flows from these and evaluates progress. A **programme approach** is most likely to promote inclusiveness in tackling the key policy areas for the Parliament to address, eg. children, poverty, social exclusion, building sustainable communities, the environment, economic development, education, housing, etc. The development of action programmes has proved effective as a tool for the European Commission to drive forward action to achieve equal opportunities in member states. This approach would lend itself even more effectively to the close-knit and inter-woven policy and service delivery structure of Scotland.

21.   In brief, the Scottish Executive would determine a set of priorities based on the Parliament's core responsibilities and would require the development of **action programmes** to operate **horizontally** across subject areas.   The programme would be developed and overseen by a **working party** which would draw together MSPs and experts from organisations sponsored by the Parliament and others. This would be an opportunity to ensure that private, public and voluntary sector interests are represented and that the views of women, black and ethnic minority people, disabled people and other previously excluded groups are heard. The action programme would set priorities for action, determine timescales and identify potential partners. In addition it would be able to require that its programme priorities were identified within budgets and priorities held by subject Committees, and in budgets allocated by sponsored bodies. This would enable the Parliament   to co-ordinate and encourage activities on the ground through   the organisations it sponsors.

22.   This approach encourages private/ public sector partnerships, voluntary and statutory sector partnerships, makes optimum use of a range of funding programmes, and is easy to monitor and evaluate. It allows for clear and visible objectives and priorities to be set and enables the public to see the progress that is achieved in a more tangible way than the simple setting of targets. Definable timescales allow for new priorities to be set and resources to be freed as progress is made.

23.   **An Equal Opportunities Action Programme:**   As well as ensuring that its policies and legislation promote equality, the Parliament will need to undertake a proactive programme to tackle inequality. The European Commission has successfully driven forward its equality agenda with a series of 3-year Equal Opportunities Action Programmes. The Parliament should draw up a similar programme for Scotland, in consultation with appropriate bodies. This would be overseen by a working party with representation from external statutory and voluntary bodies as well as MSPs.

24.   **Monitoring progress:**   The Parliament should produce annual reports on its progress towards equality. If it adopts the Programme approach it will have the basis from which the impact of its activities can be assessed. However, the setting of priorities and determining of progress both for the Parliament and for the bodies it funds will not be possible without the **disaggregation of all data by gender, ethnicity and disability.** The Parliament's responsibilities are areas of public policy and service delivery where, if equality considerations are not central to planning and policy development, there could be potential, however unintended, for discrimination to occur.   Some services are used disproportionately by women and disabled people and have a greater impact on women than on men. There are also services which ethnic minority people find difficult to access. It is, therefore, important that the Parliament be required to ensure that all data is disaggregated by gender and race and, if possible, disability, to enable the Equal Opportunities Committee to monitor progress and ensure the promotion of equality through all the Parliament's functions.

Recommendations:

- **That the Standing Orders establish a framework for debate and problem solving that avoids aggressive and sectarian debate.**

- **That Standing Orders require inclusive language, avoiding gender specific words in the spoken and written business of the Parliament and ensuring that language that may offend is unacceptable in debate.**

- **That the Parliament generally adopt a programme approach to issues which it needs to progress and that it establish an Equal Opportunities Action Programme as a matter of priority after consultation with outside statutory and voluntary organisations.**

- **Collection of all data includes disaggregation by gender, ethnicity and disability wherever possible.**

The Parliament and its Partners

25.   **Organisations the Parliament funds or contracts with:** The Parliament can use its influence and work with partners for the promotion of equal opportunities across the range of its areas of responsibilities and where it contracts services to others. It must require the highest equality standards from the bodies that it funds and sponsors. These will include the quangos within the Parliament's control, local authorities, voluntary organisations and any other bodies the Parliament establishes. The EOC wishes to see the Parliament require that any body it funds, or with which it has a contractual relationship, be required to provide evidence of an effective equal opportunities policy and to demonstrate

that the activities for which Parliament funding is required will further this policy. Funded bodies should be required to provide data on their services to the public. There are already many precedents for such an approach, including the European Union structural funds and community programmes, National Lotteries Board, and many more.

26.   As well as the bodies it sponsors, the Parliament will have a relationship with a range of public bodies operating within Scotland. The EOC notes the provision of powers to require these bodies to report to the Parliament from time to time on their activities and suggests that they should be scrutinised on progress in promoting equal opportunities through the delivery of services in Scotland.

27.   **Voluntary organisations:** The EOC works closely with a wide range of voluntary organisations in Scotland, including SCVO, STUC, women's voluntary organisations and other organisations working to promote equality of opportunity in its broadest sense. The EOC supports the formation of a Forum representing voluntary interests but stresses the need for any consultative forum to be fully inclusive of Scottish society, encompassing black and ethnic minority women and men, people with disabilities, and women and men from other previously excluded groups.

Recommendations:

- **Any organisation which the Parliament funds and sponsors should be required to provide evidence of an equal opportunities policy, demonstrate how its activities promote equality and provide data for monitoring purposes.**

- **The Parliament should ensure that its partnerships and support for the voluntary sector encompass organisations representing the needs of black and ethnic minority people, disabled people and organisations representing the views of women.**

A Framework for promoting equal rights in Scotland

28.   Although the EOC will continue to be sponsored by the DfEE, as the statutory body charged with eliminating discrimination we believe that it is in the interests of the promotion of equality to establish a close working relationship with the Parliament. The EOC is keen to play a part in developing the programmes that will create a more equal Scotland. The Commission hopes to have regular contact with the Committees and officers of the Parliament, particularly the Equal Opportunities Committee, to advise on the development and assist with the monitoring of an Equal Opportunities Action Programme.

29.   The EOC is also mindful of the need to engage in debate about the establishment of a Disability Commission. The current opportunities are timely for a dialogue on an effective framework for enforcing equal rights in Scotland within the new context created by the Parliament.

Recommendation:

- **There should be a structure for regular liaison and collaboration between the Parliament and existing equality bodies.**

Conclusion

30.   The promotion of inclusiveness and equality of opportunity for all requires that equality must be integral to the infrastructure, procedures and policies of the Parliament. It must not be retained as a responsibility within only one department or Committee, but must be a mandatory consideration throughout the workings of the Parliament and its agents. Although it will be necessary to put in place a specialist unit, Committee and programme where expertise can be developed, it must be recognised that the creation of equality of opportunity is a collective responsibility, the responsibility of each MSP and each member of every Committee.

ANNEX I

FINANCIAL ISSUES ADVISORY GROUP: SUMMARY OF RECOMMENDATIONS

1.1 This Annex summarises the main conclusions reached by the Financial Issues Advisory Group (FIAG). The Group was set up the Secretary of State for Scotland in February 1998 with the task of proposing rules, procedures, Standing Orders and legislation for the handling of financial issues by the Scottish Parliament. The objective of FIAG endorsed by CSG was to ensure that the Scottish Parliament's finances are managed in a way that is open, accessible and accountable to the people of Scotland. FIAG has considered a wide range of public finance issues. Its report is also wide ranging and covers the main aspects of public finance. The report contains recommendations on the following issues:

- terminology;

- budgetary procedures;

- accounting arrangements;

- public accountability; and

- audit arrangements.

The recommendations are summarised below. The full report is being published separately.

Terminology

1.2 At the moment, the management of Central Government finances makes use of a very specialised vocabulary that has slowly developed over many years. Though there are those that find this language useful, the definitions of some of the terms used are sometimes open to debate even amongst public sector finance specialists. More importantly, the use of specialist jargon makes it difficult for lay people to understand the financial affairs of Government.

1.3 Though finance is not a subject that lends itself to simple language, FIAG recommends that the Scottish Parliament uses plain English where it is possible. In addition, FIAG recommends that the specialist terminology is replaced by the use of standard accountancy terms. FIAG hopes that these changes will make it easier for those MSPs and members of the public who do not have a financial background to understand how the financial affairs of the Scottish Parliament are managed. The FIAG report attempts to set an example by not using government accounting jargon.

BUDGETARY PROCEDURES

1.4   Having studied the budgetary procedures of Westminster and a number of overseas legislatures, FIAG has developed a possible budget framework for the Scottish Parliament. It is based on an annual procedure designed to provide the Parliament with the opportunity to scrutinise the Executive's expenditure proposals and to monitor the financial performance of the Executive, whilst at the same time providing the stability and flexibility needed by those responsible for spending public money.

1.5   Whilst the budget process will call for Plenary debates within the Parliament, many financial management functions will be co-ordinated by Parliamentary Committees. *FIAG recommends the key Committees should be as follows.*

- **Subject Committees.** FIAG expects that there will be a number of Committees responsible for specific areas of the Parliament's business such as on transport and on housing. While such Committees will primarily be involved in policy development, they will also have an interest in financial matters. For example, subject Committees will probably wish to make recommendations on spending priorities and to consider value for money reports that concern their area.

- **Finance Committee.** The Finance Committee should be responsible for addressing overall budget priorities and for the presentation of budgets. It will be required to consider the views of Subject Committees and individual MSPs as well as the expenditure proposals of the Executive, from whom it should be independent. The Finance Committee's conclusions should form the basis of Plenary debate on budget matters, the results of which in time should inform the Executive plans.

- **Audit Committee.** The Audit Committee should also be independent of the Executive. It should take the lead in considering financial audit reports on those spending bodies that are accountable to Parliament. These include the Departments of the Executive itself, NDPBs and Health Service bodies. It should also consider vfm reports that cut across different subject areas. At times it will be necessary to consider these reports jointly with the relevant Subject Committee.

The Budget Process

1.6   FIAG's general aim has been to propose a process that will be less dominated by the Executive than is presently the case. This should enable the people of Scotland and their elected representatives to have more of a say in setting priorities for expenditure. The main report covers this aspect of FIAG's recommendations in more detail; but the process recommended by FIAG is based on three stages. It is designed to provide a timetable around which constructive dialogue between the Parliament and the Executive can take place with the objective of agreeing a budget for the year ahead **before** it begins. The stages are as follows:

- **Stage 1.** Stage 1 in the process will be a discussion on strategic priorities for the following financial year. It cannot begin until the financial processes of the previous financial year have been concluded. It is therefore likely that this stage will start in March or April. For example, the consideration of strategic priorities for the Financial Year 2001-2002 will have to wait until Financial Year 1999-2000 is complete. Stage 1 in respect of expenditure for 2001-2002 would therefore start in April 2000.

- An important part of the Stage 1 process will be consultations with the people of Scotland. In particular, FIAG expects that a review of strategy and priorities will enable interested parties such as local authorities and pressure groups to make their case to the relevant subject Committee. Committees will therefore need to set aside resources to deal with this aspect of their work.

- FIAG recommends that Stage 1 should be based on consideration of the Executive's annual report. This document, which would be published by 20 April, would outline budget proposals for the current financial year and provisional plans for the following two financial years. It would provide the basis for discussion by subject and the Finance Committee and a subsequent Plenary debate which would inform the development of detailed budget proposals by the Executive.

- **Stage 2.** FIAG recommends that Stage 2 of the process should begin with the Executive publishing a preliminary draft budget for the financial year ahead. The figures may be subject to later change, if for instance, (as may be the case) Westminster takes decisions in November that will affect the size of the total budget. Stage 2 would be a more detailed discussion on spending priorities, etc than was possible in Stage 1. It would enable MSPs to comment on the detail of proposals, and put forward alternatives. The process could lead to the publication by the Finance Committee of a report on the Executive's proposals which could then be debated in Plenary. The recommendations from this debate could then be taken into account by the Executive in its detailed budget proposals which would be ready by January.

- **Stage 3.** FIAG recommends that the Scottish Parliament should aim to complete this (largely formal) part of the process some weeks before the new financial year begins. This is to help local authorities, grant-aided bodies, etc who will wish to finalise their own plans. FIAG recommends that Stage 3 should be based on the consideration of a detailed budget which should have been published by the Executive by 20 January. The budget should have taken into account Parliament's views made at Stage 2 of the process. However it should not be mandatory for the Executive's proposals merely to follow on from these previously prepared. New proposals could, if necessary, also be submitted at this stage. Consideration would entail, amongst other things, a Plenary debate on the proposals. There will also need to be a prior vote on the Tax Varying Power if its use has been proposed by the Executive.

- During Stage 3, there will be opportunities for the Executive to amend its proposals. However, FIAG recommends that non-governmental amendments are prohibited at this time - these should be made during stages 1 and 2 when there will be better opportunities to debate fully the Executive's spending proposals. Stage 3 therefore will primarily be concerned with obtaining formal Parliamentary approval for a budget that should be in accordance with the priorities indicated by Parliament at Stages 1 and 2. However, even at this stage, Committees should be able to seek clarification from officials and the Executive. At Stage 3, the Parliament should either decide to accept or to reject the proposals that have been made.

1.7   The process that FIAG is recommending will therefore promote more public involvement and much more scrutiny by Parliament of the Executive's spending proposals than is presently the practice under the Westminster system. It is also designed to ensure that no expenditure takes place without the authority of Parliament. These procedures should not however be seen as an opportunity to rely on financial procedures alone. Instead, FIAG recommends that the Parliament's Standing Orders make sure that spending can only take place when financial legislation and policy legislation (giving the underlying authority to spend) are *both* in place.

1.8   Although it is important to agree a budget before the start of the new financial year, there will be times when this is not possible. FIAG therefore recommends a procedure to permit the Administration to continue in the event that Parliament has not approved the Executive's budget by the beginning of the financial year. FIAG is keen to avoid any implications of a "budget crisis" in the event that a budget is not approved on time. Therefore, FIAG recommends that in this situation, there should be a procedure to provide the Administration with sufficient funding to allow it to spend on individual programmes up to the amount actually spent in same month in the previous year until a budget has been agreed.

The Budget Documents

1.9   FIAG has considered what the formal budget documents ie the documents placed before Parliament at Stage 3 might look like in future. The Group has concluded that it would be helpful if the documents were structured to reflect the organisation of the Scottish Administration. FIAG hopes that the suggested format will be relatively easy to follow, enabling both MSPs and other interested parties to understand and comment on them. A key aspect will be the opening statement which sets out the scope of the proposed budget. This part of the budget (which is known in Westminster as the "Ambit") should be incorporated into the resulting legislation. In addition to the scope, FIAG recommends that the budget documents should be supported by a supporting narrative which should explain any points which cannot be clarified in the main budget document.

1.10   FIAG has considered the amount of detail that should be contained in the budget documents. The Group concluded that information should be disaggregated to the lowest level that is compatible with the need to maintain an overall picture and to avoid constraining the Executive's spending flexibility.

Changes During the Year

1.11   No matter how carefully the Executive prepares its budget, there will always be a requirement to change spending plans as the year develops. FIAG has therefore prepared a framework around which in-year changes can be made. The intention has been to develop a process which is easy to understand, that provides for effective scrutiny by Parliament but that also gives the Executive the flexibility needed to make best use of the funds that are available. FIAG proposes that the Executive should be able to move up to 15% or £50m (whichever is smaller) of the funds allocated to a Budget Section (one level below main programme in a Departmental Budget) without seeking Parliamentary approval. Transfers between Budget Subheads (subdivisions of a Budget Section) should be unrestricted. Budget transfers should, however, be reported to Parliament on a periodic basis. Transfers outwith these categories, for example, transfers between Departmental Budgets, or transfers between Budget Sections in excess of the limit, should need the authority of

Parliament. FIAG therefore recommends that procedures are put in place that would enable the Executive to seek authority routinely for budget transfers.

1.12 FIAG recommends that the documentation of budget transfers should be sufficiently clear as to permit meaningful scrutiny by the Parliament. In particular, the transfer proposals should contain information on expenditure to date so that the Parliament can consider the effectiveness of the money that has already been spent on the programme concerned.

1.13 FIAG has concluded that expenditure proposals and performance should be monitored on an annual basis. However FIAG recommends that Administration managers who make savings in one financial year should (in most circumstances) be able to retain these funds and spend them later on. This, FIAG believes, will encourage managers to seek the best possible return on their investments and will discourage profligate spending at the end of the financial year as managers attempt to use up their allocated budget. Any sums carried forward under end year flexibility arrangements would need to be included in budget approvals, or more likely, as budget amendments in the following year.

1.14 Similarly FIAG recommends that managers should be encouraged to make the most of appropriate income-generating opportunities. Consequently, the Group has concluded that in general revenue generated by programme managers should be credited to the area concerned so that increased levels of expenditure can be sustained. However, one-off receipts from the sale of capital assets (perhaps above a specified limit) should be subject to different controls and revenue from such activities should be given up.

Financial Legislation

1.15 FIAG has already referred in paragraph 1.7 to the need to ensure that expenditure should only take place when policy legislation has been followed up with appropriate financial legislation. In addition, FIAG has considered what type of financial legislation will be needed. The Group has concluded that the annual budget should be approved by means of primary legislation. This is necessary if the Executive's spending proposals are to be properly scrutinised before they are authorised. However, there are concerns that the use of primary legislation for this purpose could result in unwanted delays in agreeing the budget. FIAG is therefore recommending that the Parliament develops Standing Orders that will modify the procedures used (eg on the tabling of non-government amendments) for progressing financial legislation. This is to ensure that the budget proposals are given proper scrutiny but are not subject to unnecessary delay. Changes to expenditure limits during the financial year should, FIAG thinks, be made using secondary legislation.

ACCOUNTING ARRANGEMENTS

Resource Accounting and Budgeting

1.16 Westminster is in a process of moving away from a cash-based system of accounting to a system of "resource accounting and budgeting" (RAB) which is based on accruals accounting principles as practised by most private sector organisations in the UK. This is intended to encourage the Parliament and Executive to consider the real level of resources used instead of merely looking at the amount of cash spent each year. Local authority accounts will however continue not to be submitted to Parliament.

1.17 FIAG has given some thought to the relative merits of cash and resource based systems and has concluded that RAB gives a better overall picture than is possible when using a cash based system. Therefore FIAG recommends that the Scottish Parliament adopts RAB. There is however a timing issue here because UK government departments will not be fully implementing RAB until the Financial Year 2001-2002. The Scottish Office however, has already begun to develop its resource accounting capability and is due to produce fully audited accounts in a resource account format for the Financial Year 1999-2000, during which time the Scottish Parliament and Executive will come into being.

1.18 FIAG has concluded that it would not be logical for the Parliament to implement RAB at the same time as Whitehall because this would mean operating for a while on a cash basis. Therefore, FIAG recommends that, wherever possible, the Scottish Parliament and Executive start with RAB systems. This will require the use of both resource-based and cash figures, though resource accounts themselves will include cash figures on each Department's annual level of expenditure.

Publication of Accounts

1.19 FIAG recommends that quality standards for accounts should be considered. The Group has concluded that the following reports should be published.

1.20 An interim report by each department and agency of the Scottish Administration should be issued within two months of the financial year end. This should contain performance management information on the financial year that has just drawn to a close. These reports would inform Stage 1 of the budget planning process (see paragraph 1.6 above).

1.21 Full departmental and agency accounts (in resource format) should then be produced and submitted to Parliament at the earliest possible date.

1.22 A consolidated account (also in resource format) should then be submitted by the Executive by the end of December. This information would then be available to MSPs during Stage 3 of the budget planning process (see paragraph 1.6 above).

ACCOUNTABILITY

1.23 The Scottish Administration has to be accountable to Parliament for its use of public money. Westminster has a well-established system of "Accounting Officers" which enables the Parliament to hold senior officials accountable for the actions of their staff. FIAG thinks that a similar system should be set up in Scotland. FIAG recommends that the head of the Scottish Administration is automatically designated as the "Principal Accountable Officer" and that he or she should nominate other senior officials to be Accountable Officers for their own areas of the Administration. These individuals will be answerable to the Parliament normally through subject Committees and/or the Audit Committee for their actions. FIAG also recommends that arrangements are put in place to permit managers with specific responsibility for an issue under review to attend Committees when their presence (in addition to or instead of) an Accountable Officer would be helpful.

1.24 In the past, the system of Accounting Officers has concentrated on examining officials when it appears that something may have gone awry. FIAG recommends that in future, the system of Accountable Officers is used as much to share examples of good practice as it is to establishing an error has taken place.

AUDIT ARRANGEMENTS

1.25 FIAG has made a number of recommendations on the audit of those areas of the public sector accountable to the people of Scotland. Much of the responsibility for these will fall to the Audit Committee whose role has been set out at paragraph 1.5. This body will consider reports presented by the Auditor General for Scotland (AGS) and should take the lead in making sure that standards of regularity and propriety are exemplary amongst those organisations that report to it. In addition, FIAG sees the Audit Committee as having a key role alongside subject Committees in making sure that the people of Scotland receive the best possible value for money in return for their investments.

Auditor General for Scotland

1.26 The Scotland Act makes provision for the appointment of an Auditor General for Scotland (AGS) who will be both independent of the Scottish Parliament and the Executive. He or she will be responsible for the commissioning of financial and value for money audit across much of the public sector in Scotland. (Local authorities will continue to be audited by auditors appointed by the Accounts Commission; and these audit reports will not be submitted to Parliament.) FIAG is recommending that the appointment of an AGS should be an early and important task for the Parliament.

Audit Delivery

1.27 At present the bulk of the public sector in Scotland is audited either by the National Audit Office (NAO) or auditors appointed by the Accounts Commission. FIAG is of the view that the public sector in Scotland does not justify two main audit organisations. The Group is therefore recommending a merger between the audit staff of the Accounts Commission and NAO (Scotland) into a new audit provider to be known as "Audit Scotland". This organisation will be able to supply audit services to the AGS (who will also serve as the Chief Executive of Audit Scotland) and to the Accounts Commission, both of whom will also be able to procure audits from private sector providers.   The establishment of Audit Scotland is a significant task and FIAG recommends that plans for this are developed at the earliest possible opportunity.

1.28 At present the statutory audit of financial statements, and value for money studies are integrated as much as the specialised nature of these two different tasks allows. FIAG recommends that this arrangement should continue. The Group has also concluded that audit reports should be signed off by the organisation that undertakes each audit rather than by the AGS (or the Accounts Commission) who procures it.   Audits should, where appropriate, contain an opinion as to whether or not the audited body has achieved the performance targets set and reported on by its managers, using the performance indicators chosen by the audited body. These comments should not however extend to expressing an opinion on the targets themselves. (FIAG does however accept that in the local government sector separate arrangements exist for the setting of national performance standards and that these should continue.)

Appointment of Auditors and Rights of Access

1.29 As far as audit arrangements are concerned, the public sector in Scotland can be broken down into 3 main areas:

- central Government bodies;

- public bodies, including local authorities, receiving grants from Ministers; and

- local spending bodies.

1.30 FIAG has made a number of recommendations about the rights of access and explanation that the auditors of these organisations should enjoy. The Group has also considered the possibility of changing the audit arrangements for some of these bodies so that in future, their audits are commissioned by the AGS.

1.31 FIAG commends to the Scottish Parliament, the Public Audit Model as developed by the Public Audit forum. This Model sets out independent arrangements for the appointment of auditors and lays down guidelines for audit practice. It should be applied to all areas within the Parliament's competence as follows:

- Central Government Bodies: Legislation should put in place arrangements for the audit of central Government bodies by auditors appointed by the AGS. FIAG recommends that in doing so, the Parliament enshrines the right of access to and explanation of, any documents as may reasonably be required when undertaking a financial or value for money audit.

- Public bodies receiving grants from Ministers: The current audit arrangements for these organisations are mixed. Local authorities and health boards are audited by auditors appointed by the Accounts Commission. Audits of NDPBs may be carried out by the NAO or by auditors appointed by the Secretary of State, company members or (in the case of further education colleges) by governing bodies. FIAG has recommended at paragraph 1.33 that all audit appointments for the Health Service should be made by the AGS. The Group also recommends that, where possible, the AGS should also appoint auditors for Executive NDPBs set up under statute. FIAG accepts that the Parliament will not be able to change the arrangements for appointing auditors for bodies set up under general legislation, such as the Companies Acts. Auditors should also be granted statutory rights of access to the records of the NDPBs and health service bodies concerned. The separate arrangements for local authorities should continue.

- Local spending bodies: These organisations (such as universities, housing associations and local enterprise companies) receive money from the Scottish Consolidated Fund second hand through funding bodies. Again the audit arrangements are mixed. FIAG recommends that the arrangements should be made more consistent and that the AGS should be granted statutory rights of access to any local spending body that is significantly dependant on public funds or statutory levies.

1.32 There are likely to be times when the Executive will employ contractors to carry out activities on its behalf. The Executive must be able to ensure that it received good value for money when purchasing a service. When necessary, the contractual arrangements should make provision for access to the contractor's relevant records. However, there should be no overall statutory provision for this.

NHS Audit

1.33 At present the NHS consolidated accounts are audited by the Comptroller and Auditor General whilst the audit of NHS Trusts and Boards is commissioned by the Accounts Commission, which does not report to Parliament. Whilst this arrangement has been cost-effective, FIAG thinks there are strong arguments for audit reports on the NHS being made to the Parliament. This is consistent with the lines of democratic accountability. This points to auditors being appointed by the AGS. Moreover, having the Accounts Commission reporting on locally elected bodies and the AGS on expenditure under the Scottish Executive would recognise the different position of locally elected bodies. It would also, amongst other things, help to resolve the present *perception* of duplication of audit effort in the NHS. For these reasons, FIAG recommends that in future, the AGS should have sole responsibility for commissioning audits in the NHS.

Public Audit Commission

1.34 FIAG is of the view that a small Public Audit Commission should be established by the Scottish Parliament. This Commission would not be able to direct the work of the AGS (who must have guaranteed independence both from Parliament and the Executive) but instead would consider general questions of accountability and audit, such as the resources that the Parliament should allocate to audit. It would also appoint auditors for the AGS and for Audit Scotland.

OTHER ISSUES

Contingent liabilities

1.35 The Westminster Parliament has established conventions to limit the ability of Ministers to enter, without informing Parliament, into agreements with outside bodies that might result in future expenditure. FIAG concludes that the Scottish Parliament should make similar arrangements and recommends that the Executive must obtain authority from the Scottish Parliament before entering into any agreement that might result in subsequent spending in excess of £1m.

The Resource Consequences of Policy Legislation

1.36 New policy legislation often results in additional expenditure commitments. FIAG recommends that legislative proposals contain as full statements as possible on the resource implications so that the Parliament can consider the full ramifications of any decision. Where opposition or backbench amendments have resource implications, these too should be made plain.

Temporary spending power for the Executive

1.37 The Parliament will on occasion face requests for additional funding to support sudden unexpected needs. In most cases, this will be a question of providing additional support to existing programmes. FIAG recommends that Parliament set aside a Contingency Reserve for this purpose.

1.38 At times, the Executive will seek to spend money on areas for which legislation does not exist. A procedure is required to enable spending to take place on a temporary basis until Parliament is able to authorise the expenditure. FIAG recommends that procedures are developed to facilitate this process and that a separate Contingency Fund is set up, from which money can be drawn by the Executive on a temporary basis.

Arrangements for the Scottish Parliamentary Corporate Body

1.39 The Scottish Parliamentary Corporate Body will be responsible for the administration of the Parliament itself. Its budget should therefore be set in a way that respects both the rights of the Parliament and the Executive, within a framework of transparency and openness to the Scottish people.

Monitoring and control of administrative expenditure

1.40 FIAG has concluded that it would be helpful if the Parliament is able to scrutinise the level of the Executive's administrative expenditure.   Therefore the Group recommends arrangements are put in place that will enable the Parliament to ascertain the levels of administrative expenditure being incurred in the various business units of the Scottish Administration.

LIST OF FIAG'S RECOMMENDATIONS

Terminology

1. In future, Government accounting should use simple language and community understood terms.

BUDGETARY PROCEDURES

2. The Scottish Parliament should adopt an annual procedure to scrutinise and approve the expenditure proposals of the Executive.

Committees

3. The Scottish Parliament should use a structure based on 3 Committee types. These are: Subject Committee, the Finance Committee and the Audit Committee.

Parliamentary Consideration

4. The whole Parliament should have the opportunity to scrutinise Budget Proposals and Budget amendments. The Subject and Finance Committee might also play an important role in scrutiny of the Executive's main budget proposals prior to consideration by the Plenary.

5. It should also be open to members to use forms of questions or enquiries although it is acknowledged that this is probably more effective in calling the Government to account in relation to policy questions than for specialised financial scrutiny.

Parliamentary controls through budget procedures

6. The Scottish Parliament should adopt broad principles as follows:

- budget approval should be by way of primary legislation;

- there should be no expenditure without appropriation legislation;

- revised budgets are produced to reflect adjustments;

- no undue reliance on Budget approvals for providing underlying powers to undertake functions;

- an absolute (cash) limit to spending;

- annuality of agreed budget sums (but with arrangements to provide sensible carry forward);

- separate authority needed for overspends;

- emergency spending subject to Parliament's authority;

- no release of funds without legislative authority; and

- Parliamentary authority is required to apply receipts.

7. There should be a presumption that the flexibility to carry forward savings from one financial year to another should be passed to programme managers in order to influence management behaviour.

8. FIAG supports a regime (approved by the Parliament) which enables programme managers to retain current receipts to add to programme expenditure. A procedure will be required to decide which receipts should be available to sustain increased expenditure and which should be surrendered. Capital receipts above certain limits to be decided should be controlled.

Three Stage Framework

9. *FIAG recommends a 3 Stage framework for budgeting approval*:

- Stage 1 – A discussion of future strategy and priorities with public input through subject Committees. Debate to be supported by the Executive's publication of an annual report by 20 April setting out budget proposals for the year immediately ahead and provisional plans for two further years. The report should also cover policy objectives and some assessment of performance against past objectives.

- Stage 2 - Consideration of draft budget proposals by the Executive taking account of the outcome of Committees' considerations at Stage 1. Parliament would have the option of proposing an alternative budget, not involving more money in total than the Executive's proposals. This would not be binding on the Executive.

- Stage 3 - Consideration of the Executive's final budget proposals leading to approval or rejection by the Parliament by the start of the financial year.

Budget Documentation

10. Budgets are formal procedures but are nevertheless necessary in terms of securing the Parliament's formal authority for expenditure and as a means for checking the regularity of payments, etc.

11. Budgets should follow the internal structure of the Scottish Administration and hence align with Accountable Officer responsibilities.

12. The ambit is a useful concept and should be retained. However, FIAG recommends that this part of a Budget should be known as its "Scope" as this is a term which is more commonly understood.

13. The Budget spending proposals should cover all expenditure by the Executive which the Parliament has to approve, rather than all public expenditure in Scotland.

14. These proposals should also include, after consultation with the Parliament, expenditure which the Parliament has to approve but is not formally for the Executive to propose - notably expenditure by the Parliament itself and expenditure on judges' salaries.

15.   The Executive should also report to the Parliament on the levels or expected levels of other public expenditure in Scotland, including expenditure decisions by local authorities, expenditure by Parliament and judges' salaries.

16.   Each Budget proposal should be accompanied by a narrative (ie a financial memorandum) explaining the objectives which would set out proposed outputs and expected outcomes.

17.   Budgets should be disaggregated to a lower level than that required by the Parliament for the purposes of financial control.

Interim spending approval

18.   The Scottish Parliament should be invited to adopt an interim budget approval procedure to be used if the Parliament did not formally approve the Budget before the start of the financial year.

In-year changes

19.   The Parliament should adopt arrangements that balance in-year flexibility for managers with Parliamentary control.

20.   Budget amendments should:

- be simpler to understand;

- provide more opportunities to present Budget amendments to Parliament if required;

- provide monitoring information in relation to expenditure; and

- provide better dovetailing between control mechanisms and statutory approvals.

Executive discretion in relation to in-year changes

21.   The Executive should be allowed reasonable discretion to transfer funds with appropriate internal controls but they should be subject to the Parliament being informed of transfers on a regular basis and not just when accounts are prepared as now.

22.   Budget transfers should be allowed between sections or subheads of a Departmental Budget but not between Departmental Budgets.

23.   Departments should be allowed to automatically transfer up to 15% of receiving subheads or £50m whichever is the lesser.

24.   The system for budget transfers should be reviewed in 2002.

Primary versus Secondary Legislation

25.   FIAG recommends Standing Orders are developed to enable financial legislation to be passed more quickly than is normally the case eg by limiting opportunities for non-Government amendments.

26.   In addition:

- the Executive should give as much information as early as possible on proposals for use of the tax varying power;

- amendments by MSPs should be restricted to expenditure proposals (and should not include revenue or taxes);

- budget approval should be made using primary legislation; and

- in the event of Parliament rejecting the entire budget, fresh proposals must be brought forward before the expiry of the interim spending approval.

ACCOUNTING ARRANGEMENTS

27.   The Scottish Parliament should adopt resource accounting and budgeting.

28.   Resource budgeting should be implemented one year earlier than the Whitehall model as far as is practicable.

29.   The Scottish Administration should provide a clear explanation, perhaps in a supporting memorandum of how the numbers in accounts differ from those that would have appeared in the old style cash accounts and how they relate to the (cash) sum paid into the Scottish Consolidated Fund by the UK Government.

Style and presentation of accounts

30.   Accounts should be produced to cover all Government expenditure in Scotland.

31.   In addition, separate work should be undertaken to distil these into more accessible versions.

32.   A comparison with the previous financial year should be provided. This should be wide-ranging and cover financial and performance information.

33.   Performance reporting will be an important part of resource accounting; and annual reports should be important. These should set out overall commentary on:

- the overall budget strategy;

- the nature and objectives of each main programme;

- the outturns in previous years, including assessments of output and performance against objectives as well as financial outturns;

- the plans for the year ahead, as approved by Parliament; and

- the provisional plans for the two subsequent years.

34.   FIAG recommends that separate volumes should be issued for each of the Executive's spending Departments.

Timing issues

35. The Scottish Parliament should set a statutory deadline of 31 December by which the preceding year's accounts must be published. Departments and the Auditor General might be invited to make progress against a target.

36. Executive Agency and (Scottish) Departmental Resource Accounts should be produced at the earlier possible date, ahead of the Consolidated Resource Account.

37. An interim report should be provided to the Parliament in May containing performance management information in relation to the financial year which will have just drawn to a close. The intention is that this information would inform the Scottish Parliament's consideration of resource allocation decisions throughout the early summer. This could be incorporated into the Annual Report that sets out the Executive's budget plans for the financial year ahead.

ACCOUNTABILITY

38. The Scottish Parliament should set up a similar system to that of "Accounting Officers" as used at by the UK Parliament. Senior officials within the Scottish Administration should be designated as "Accountable Officers". This term reflects more accurately the role such individuals would have in being accountable to the Parliament for the actions of the Scottish Administration. (Although the term "Accounting Officer" is well understood in Government circles it tends to indicate a more specialist financial role and is hence somewhat misleading to the lay person.) FIAG recommends that the head of the Scottish Administration is automatically designated as Principal Accountable Officer on appointment. He or she should then be responsible for appointing other Accountable Officers throughout the rest of the Administration. These officials could then be required to account for the actions of the Administration both to the Audit Committee and to any subject Committee considering a value for money report produced by the AGS.

39. FIAG recommends a mechanism whereby Committees are able to liaise with the Administration to ensure that, in addition to or instead of the Accountable Officer concerned, other relevant officials can be called to give evidence.

40. The system of accountability should be seen as a way of promoting a free flow of information between Parliament and the Administration and the sharing of good practice should be an integral part of the process.

AUDIT ARRANGEMENTS

Role of Committees in relation to audit

41. Vfm issues should be dealt with by the Audit Committee, on Subject Committee or a combination of the two as is appropriate.

42. The Auditor General should co-ordinate the programme and (as set out in statute), consult as appropriate.

43. Recommendations of Committee should not be binding on the Executive but the Executive should be required to publish a response within a specified timescale (FIAG recommends two months) and should be required to report progress on the actions that have been agreed.

Statutory audit of financial statements

44.   The Scottish Parliament should be invited to set out in statute equivalent arrangements (to those at Westminster) for the audit of financial statements, together with a timetable for their presentation.

Audit of Regularity and Propriety

45.   The Scottish Parliament should be invited to set out in statute a role for the Auditor General for Scotland in examining issues of regularity and propriety in public expenditure.

Performance Management

46.   The auditor's new role should include the validation of performance measures within the context of financial audit and vfm work.

47.   Auditors should be entitled to comment whether indicators that have been set are appropriate and complete in relation to policy objectives but they should not set indicators.

Audit Approach

48.   The AGS should be invited to continue the development of good practice in public audit in Scotland.

Rights of access

49.   The Scottish Parliament should be invited to legislate to afford the AGS an explicit right to require explanation as well as the right of access to documents of the Scottish Administration.

50.   Existing audit arrangements for public bodies receiving grants from Ministers should be made more consistent by making the AGS or his appointee the statutory auditor for executive NDPBs, where this is within the competence of the Scottish Parliament.

51.   There should be a statutory right of access for the AGS to all public bodies receiving funds directly or indirectly from the Scottish Consolidated Fund including public sector companies, with the exception of local authorities for whom separate arrangements should continue to apply.

52.   Legislation should provide a consistent statutory right of access to the AGS to all local spending bodies, subject to any body being significantly dependent for its income from public funds or statutory levies.

53.   When access to the records of contractors is required, this should be agreed during contract negotiations.

Delivery of audit functions

54.   The Parliament should continue an audit arrangement which integrates financial audit and VFM.

55.   The current staff of NAO in Scotland and the Accounts Commission should be merged to form one audit delivery agency, Audit Scotland.

56.   The Auditor General's role should encompass the responsibilities of the Chief Executive of Audit Scotland.

57.   There should be safeguards to protect the legitimate and distinctive interest of the Accounts Commission and the Controller of Audit.

58.   There should be a single central support service unit, separate from Audit Scotland, reporting to the AGS, the Accounts Commission and the Controller of Audit. Either party would be able to withdraw from this arrangement if they had concerns about the unit's independence or effectiveness.

59.   FIAG recommends a working group to look at the issues involving in setting up Audit Scotland.   The early appointment of the AGS would help this process.

Appointment of the Auditor General for Scotland

60.   The AGS should be appointed as early as possible.

61.   Recruitment should be through open competition.

62.   The criteria to be used in selecting the candidates should be published and should be included in the advertisement and particulars of the post.

63.   A panel should be appointed to deal with the matter. It should be chaired by the Presiding Officer, who will appoint the other members of the panel having regard to overall party mix.   The panel should include the respective chairs of the Public Accounts Commission and the Audit Committee. The Parliament should consider whether to include in its arrangements for the appointment of independent assessors to the panel.

64.   Selection procedures should reflect Nolan principles.

65.   The Parliament should set a salary for the AGS that is commensurate with similar posts elsewhere in the UK.

Public Accounts Commission

66.   There should be a Public Accounts Commission, which would consist of Members of the Scottish Parliament.   It would have commissioning and funding responsibilities in relation to public accounts.

OTHER ISSUES

Contingent Liabilities

67.   There should be a constraint on the Executive's ability to enter into contingent liabilities, and the Scottish Parliament may wish to consider a limit, above which prior approval must be sought.   It should be considerably higher than Westminster precedent.

Resource consequences of policy legislation

68.   There should be standing orders that would require the Executive to provide, for all legislative proposals, as full a statement as possible on their resource implications,

including timescales and margins of uncertainty. The information should also distinguish the implications for local government and compliance costs. This statement should be developed and scrutinised as part of the pre-legislative process.

69. Any opposition or backbench amendments to policy Bills having significant additional resource consequences should be subject to a special scrutiny procedure.

Temporary spending power of the Executive

70. Parliament should make arrangements to set aside each year, a reserve. This would consist of money that will be held back to deal with any crises that arise.

71. The Parliament should make arrangements for a Contingencies Fund to cope with the need to spend money on areas where there is no authority for expenditure. The Parliament's fixed budget is distinct from the arrangement at Westminster, and therefore, the Scottish Executive should be limited in the amount of advance it can access and also the time it has to report to Parliament and secure approval.

72. Normally, the Finance Committee (or sub-Committee/chair) should ratify Contingencies Fund expenditure in advance (except during the recess).

73. The use of Contingencies Fund is to be disclosed, even if the Scottish Parliament is in recess and a report made to the Finance Committee as soon as possible.

Scottish Parliamentary Corporate Body

74. FIAG believes that it is in the public interest that the Parliament designate an Accountable Officer in respect of the SPCB expenditure.

75. FIAG recommends that, in common with other Parliaments, there should be some special procedures for determining how much money the Parliament spends on its own administration and on public audit.

Monitoring and control of administrative expenditure

76. A single administration budget should be established for all core Departments' expenditure or administration.

77. For information purposes, administration expenditure should be disaggregated as far as possible to individual Departments, with planned and actual expenditure shown in their budgeting and reporting arrangements.

78. Distinct business units, such as Executive Agencies, should have a discrete budget with the Chief Officer of the body concerned being accountable to the Parliament for that budget. These organisations should have the discretion to manage their budget within the overall limits set by Parliament, subject to the general rules for switching resources within a budget. They should in principle be able to retain excess current receipts and use these to finance any new expenditure, including expenditure on administration.

79. The Executive should bring forward detailed proposals for internal controls over expenditure on administration, and these should be reported to Parliament along with the Executive's proposals for the use of delegations.

Detailed oversight of financial procedures

80.   FIAG recommends detailed guidance is developed on financial procedures. However, normally it should not be necessary for the Parliament to be burdened with this. The Audit Committee should nevertheless receive copies of all guidance on which it could comment/amend if it chose.

MSP Training

81.   FIAG recommends the SPCB develops a financial briefing package which will enable new MSPs quickly to gain a thorough understanding of how the Parliament's financial affairs are likely to be managed.

ANNEX J

EXPERT PANEL ON INFORMATION AND COMMUNICATIONS TECHNOLOGIES: SUB-GROUP ON DEMOCRATIC PARTICIPATION: SUMMARY OF RECOMMENDATIONS

1. The Scottish Parliament should establish a process to review, report and make recommendations to improve democratic participation.

2. The Scottish Parliament should create a Citizen's Charter committing all MSPs and officials to best customer care models of practice.

3. The Scottish Parliament should take account of the variable nature of individuals and organisations needing public information and make appropriate provision.

4. The Scottish Parliament should develop non-technology based public information media to cater for the needs of the information, economic and technology have-nots.

5. The Scottish Parliament should seek to encourage and engage young people in schools, colleges and universities in the work of the Parliament.

6. The Scottish Parliament should also use similar, though less formal, initiatives to continually encourage the population in lifelong learning about the workings of the Parliament.

7. The Scottish Parliament should appoint an Education Officer, with an education background, who should be responsible for developing for adults and children:

- interactive CD-ROM education courses;

- Internet Web-site education pages;

- content for inclusion in school, college and university curricula;

- an education visits programme for the Scottish Parliament campus.

8. The Scottish Parliament should establish partnerships with educational organisations in Scotland, such as the Scottish Consultative Council on the Curriculum and the Scottish Virtual Teachers Centre, to develop educational materials and ensure their inclusion in curricula.

9. The Scottish Parliament should ensure background papers, statistics, etc should be clearly indexed for research purposes including research by interest groups and should be easily accessible on the Internet.

10. The Scottish Parliament should provide a room for research associated with the Parliament for physical inspection of documents.

11.   The Scottish Parliament should make educational materials relating to the Scottish Parliament available in public libraries and on the Internet to assist with the education of the adult population.

12.   The Scottish Parliament should establish a process to investigate, make recommendations and report on adaptive and emerging technologies which should be used to aid information flow.

13.   When the Scottish Parliament and/or individual MSPs have sought views they should "close the loop" by telling the electorate what they did with these views.

14.   The Scottish Parliament, when reporting on how consultation took place, should emphasise the quality of consultation as well as the quantity.

15.   Unless otherwise stated, the Scottish Parliament should make responses to consultation publicly available.

16.   Community media centres should be developed across Scotland where assistance is available to local communities to develop submissions to the Scottish Parliament.

17.   The Scottish Parliament should create a Citizen's Charter which should set measurable standards for information provision and responses to submissions.

18.   The Scottish Parliament should produce an annual report covering standards achieved and an action plan to improve performance.

GLOSSARY OF TERMS

Absolute majority: a number of votes equivalent to more than half of the total number of seats in the Parliament (in a Parliament with 129 seats, 65 votes would be required to obtain an absolute majority).

All-purpose Committee: Committee combining the "Standing" and "Select" Committee roles at Westminster, and which therefore undertakes Enquiries, considers legislation and scrutinises the Executive.

Clerk of the Parliament: Head Official and Chief Executive of the Parliament administration.

Clerk to a Committee: Official providing support to a Committee of the Parliament.

Convener: Chairperson of a Committee.

Derogation: Exception made for a particular group with respect to a piece of legislation.

Executive Bill: Bill proposed by the party or parties forming the Scottish Executive.

Financial Legislation: Legislation authorising the Scottish Executive to spend money.

First Minister: Head of the Scottish Executive.

Intra vires: Within the legislative competence of the Scottish Parliament.

Legislative Competence: Areas within which the Scottish Parliament can legislate under the terms of the Scotland Act 1998.

MSP: Member of the Scottish Parliament.

Non-Executive Business: Business proposed by parties who do not form part of the Scottish Executive, or by independents.

Plenary: Meeting of the full Parliament.

Presiding Officer: MSP who chairs the Plenary and is responsible for the orderly conduct of the Parliament (similar to the Speaker at Westminster).

Primary Legislation: Acts of the Scottish Parliament.

Private Legislation: Legislation promoted through the Parliament by private individuals/bodies.

Private Member's Bill: Proposed legislation introduced by an individual MSP.

Quorum: Minimum number of Members required to be present for business to be undertaken.

175

Recess: Times when the Parliament is not meeting.

Scottish Administration: Umbrella term for the Scottish Executive, junior Scottish Ministers, certain non-Ministerial officers (eg Registrar General), and their staff.

Scottish Block: Financial resources allocated each year to Scotland by Westminster.

Scottish Executive: Ministers of the new Scottish Government - a First Minister, Scottish Ministers, Lord Advocate and Solicitor General.

Junior Scottish Ministers: MSPs appointed to assist the Scottish Ministers.

Scottish Law Officers: Lord Advocate and Solicitor General.

Scottish Ministers: Ministers appointed by the First Minister, with the agreement of the Parliament and approved by Her Majesty The Queen.

Scottish Parliamentary Corporate Body (SPCB): The body which will provide the Parliament with property, services and staff.

Secondary Legislation: Legislation which can be made by the Executive and others (eg Registrar General, Courts (normally with Parliamentary approval)) implementing policy already agreed by the Parliament in an Act, or in an Act of the Westminster Parliament. Also known as Subordinate or Delegated Legislation.

Standing Orders: Rules governing the proceedings of the Parliament.

Statutory Instrument: A type of Secondary Legislation.

Subject Committee: A Committee of the Parliament whose remit will be to consider a particular policy area, and which is not one of the mandatory Committees whose remit is prescribed in Standing Orders.

Sub judice: Issue currently subject to legal proceedings.

Ultra vires: Legislation outwith the competence of the Scottish Parliament.